HEMINGWAY'S

RELIGIOUS EXPERIENCE

HEMINGWAY'S
RELIGIOUS EXPERIENCE

By

JULANNE ISABELLE

VANTAGE PRESS

New York   Washington   Hollywood

FIRST EDITION

Copyright, © 1964, by Julanne Isabelle

Published by Vantage Press, Inc.
120 West 31st Street, New York 1, N.Y.

Manufactured in the United States of America

Dedicated to Dr. Earl Hilton, Dr. Arthur Pennell, and
Associate Professor Richard Sonderegger

ACKNOWLEDGMENTS

Thanks are due to the following publishers for permission to reprint passages from the works indicated:

Atlantic-Little, Brown, and Co.: From *At the Hemingways'*, Marcelline Hemingway Sanford, copyright, 1962.

Ballantine: From *The Peace Race*, Seymour Melman, copyright, 1961. Reprinted by permission of Brandt and Brandt, New York.

Church Hymnal Corporation: From *The Book of Common Prayer*, copyright, 1945.

Crown Publishers Inc.: From *Men At War*, Ernest Hemingway, ed., copyright, 1942.

Penguin Books, Ltd., Harmondsworth, Middlesex, England; E. P. Dutton Co., New York, U.S. agents.; from *Yevtushenko, Selected Poems* by Yevgeny Yevtushenko translated by Robin-Milner-Gulland and Peter Levi, copyright, 1962.

Harcourt, Brace and World (Reynal and Hitchcock): From *On Native Ground*, Alfred Kazin, copyright, 1942.

Little, Brown and Co., Boston; from *The Poems of Emily Dickinson*, edited by Martha Dickinson Bianchi and Alfred Leete Hampson; copyright, 1930.

Princeton University Press: From *Hemingway, The Writer as Artist*, Carlos Baker, 1952.

Charles Scribner's Sons: From the writing of Ernest Hemingway, *Death in the Afternoon*, 1952, *A Farewell to Arms*, 1948, *The Fifth Column and The First 49 Stories*, 1938, *For Whom the Bell Tolls*, 1940, *Men Without Women*, 1927, *The Old Man and the Sea*, 1952, *The Sun Also Rises*, 1954, *To Have and Have Not*, 1937, and *Winner Take Nothing*, 1933.

Simon and Schuster: From *Portrait of Hemingway*, Lillian Ross, copyright, 1961.

World Publishing Co.: From *My Brother, Ernest Hemingway*, Leicester Hemingway, copyright, 1962.

Yale French Studies, No. 25, Camus Issue; copyright, 1960.

INTRODUCTION

With sincere humility and integrity I submit the religious experience of Ernest Hemingway. I have probed into the soul of a man and found beauty and courage dedicated to God.

Ernest Hemingway understood thoroughly the sermon of Qoheleth who said, To every thing there is a season, and a time to every purpose under the heaven:

A time to be born, and a time to die; a time to plant, and a
time to pluck up that which is planted;

A time to kill, and a time to heal; a time to break down and
a time to build up;

A time to weep and a time to laugh; a time to mourn and
a time to dance;

A time to cast away stones, and a time to gather stones
together; a time to embrace, and a time to refrain
from embracing;

A time to get, and a time to lose; a time to keep, and a time
to cast away;

A time to rend, and a time to sew; a time to keep silence, and
a time to speak;

A time to love and a time to hate; a time of war, and a time
of peace.—Ecclesiastes 3:1-8

Julanne Isabelle

ENCOUNTER

We were sitting about taking coffee
in the aerodrome café at Copenhagen
Where everything was brilliance and comfort
and stylish to the point of tedium.
The old man suddenly appeared
or rather happened like an event in nature
in an ordinary greenish anorak
his face scarred by the salt and burning wind
ploughing a furrow through a crowded room
and walking like a sailor from the wheel.
His beard was like the white foam of the sea,
brimming and glistening around his face.
His gruffness and his winner's certainty
sent up a wave around him as he walked
through the old fashions aping modern fashions.
He in his open collar and rough shirt
stepping aside from vermouth and pernod
stood at the bar demanding Russian Vodka
and waving away the soda with a "No."
He with the scars marking his tanned forearms
his filthy trousers and his noisy shoes
had better style than anyone in the crowd.
The solid ground seemed to quiver under
the heavy authority of that tread.
Somebody smiled across, 'Look at that!
you'd think that was Hemingway,' he said.
Expressed in details of his short gestures
and heavy motions of his fisherman's walk.

He was a statue sketched in a rough rock
one treading down bullets and centuries
one walking like a man hunched in a trench,
pushing aside people and furniture.
It was the very image of Hemingway.
(Later I heard that it was Hemingway.)

    —by Yevgeny Yevtushenko *Yevtushenko: Selected Poems* translated by Robin Milner—Gulland and Peter Levi, Penguin Books Ltd. Harmondsworth, Middlesex, England, 1962. U. S. Agent—E. P. Dutton and Co.

CONTENTS

Introduction

"Encounter" by Yevgeny Yevtushenko

CHAPTER I

HEMINGWAY'S PROTESTANT TRADITION

Between the poles of belief and disbelief lies Ernest Hemingway's religious experience. The many existing interpretations of his religious position attest to its complexity. It would therefore be impossible to fit this prodigious figure into a narrow orthodox tradition. Hemingway was a religiously oriented man whose tempered faith was forged within the framework of an American Protestant tradition, hardened by the disillusionment of war and the 1920's, and annealed within the framework of a broad, ancient Catholic tradition, constantly being tested for its tenacity and possessing the properties essential to a universal belief.

Ernest Hemingway was born in Oak Park, Illinois, on July 21, 1899, to American Protestant parents. His mother, Grace Hall Hemingway, the daughter of Ernest Hall and Carolina Hancock Hall, was an Episcopalian. His father, Clarence Edmonds Hemingway, was a Congregationalist. The Hemingway family of Oak Park were members of the First Congregational Church.

Hemingway was strongly influenced by these two Protestant beliefs which found expression through the varied members of the family. Grandfather Ernest Hall, a stern religious man whom the family affectionately called "Abba," from the Biblical phrase meaning "Father," was responsible for Ernest's Episcopalian beliefs. Influential in family devotions, Grandfather Hall often led the family in daily prayers and table grace. A typical Hemingway family blessing was, "For what we are about to receive, may the Lord make us truly thankful, for Jesus' sake. Amen." [1] Ernest, jokingly, would say this quickly, using only sounds and rhythms, for which he received harsh criticism. Grandfather Hall attended the Grace Episcopal Church every Sunday and conducted the daily devotional services at home from the book *Daily Strength for Daily Needs*. The Episcopal Service book available to the family was *The Book of Common Prayer*, which served as the source for the paraphrased title of Ernest Hemingway's first book, *in our time,* from the "Evening Prayer":

> The Lord be with you
> And with thy spirit
> Let us pray.
> O Lord, show thy mercy upon us
> And grant us thy salvation.
> O Lord, save the State
> And mercifully hear us when we call upon thee.
> Endue thy Ministers with righteousness
> And make thy chosen people joyful.
> O Lord, save thy people
> And bless thine inheritance.
> Give peace in our time, O Lord.
> For it is thou, Lord, only that makest
> Us dwell in safety.
> O God, make clean our hearts within us
> And take not thy Holy Spirit from us.[2]

Ernest admired the directness of his grandfather, whom Marcelline Hemingway Sanford remembers "kneeling with eyes uplifted praying directly to his friend, God." This directness developed in Ernest an unrelenting honesty. As a boy, Ernest listened with absorbed interest to his grandfather's accounts of courageous action in the Civil War, and later, in *For Whom the Bell Tolls*, recounts indirectly his grandfather's reaction to inhumanity. He further relates his grandfather's belief that suicide is a cowardly act in the story "Fathers and Sons." Hemingway's qualities of honesty, courage and courage of conviction are traceable to the influence of Grandfather Hall.

18

From his other grandfather, Anson Tyler Hemingway, a Congregationalist and another deeply religious man, having as his dearest friend the evangelist Dwight L. Moody, Ernest learned the value of a life of discipline and thrift. To this Episcopalian-Congregationalist foundation of the two grandfathers, Grandmother Adelaide Edmonds Hemingway[3] added a love and respect of nature in her son Clarence Edmonds Hemingway, and he, in turn, instilled a similar love in Ernest. Clarence E. Hemingway did not approach nature from a naturalist's viewpoint but from the Creator's viewpoint, preserving the Biblical concept of the creation of the world in seven days, carefully explaining that no one had set the length of the day. This knowledge of natural history was meant to supplement the truths Ernest learned in Sunday school.

Hemingway's father added a puritanical element to Ernest's evolving Protestant tradition. Clarence Edmonds Hemingway was an uncompromising man who believed strongly in the conventional American Midwestern Protestant beliefs of the day. Right was right, and wrong was wrong. He often was a stern disciplinarian, forcing the children on their knees to pray to God for forgiveness. He believed that social dancing, card playing and gambling were wrong, and he disapproved of smoking and the drinking of alcoholic beverages. And yet, though he was a thoroughly self-disciplined man, he lacked some courage of conviction and often hid behind a quick "no" in making decisions. Through the stern influence of Grandfather Hall, Ernest had adopted courage of conviction as a foremost rule of life, and he resented his father's lack of conviction on basic moral issues. He writes about it in his story, "The Doctor and the Doctor's Wife." Mrs. Hemingway was often influential in turning these quick decisions to "yes"; and Ernest's heightened resentment of the domineering influence of his mother's strong character can be felt in this story. A question of morality arises early in the story when the Indian, Dick Boulton, accuses the doctor of stealing the logs. If the doctor were firm of conviction that he was right, he would not have hesitated and walked away, but the wife places emphasis

19

on the doctor's weakness by stressing, under the blind of convention:

> "Remember, he who ruleth the spirit is greater than he who taketh the city."

She adds to his doubt, contradicting his belief that Dick Boulton was evading payment of a bill, saying:

> "Dear, I don't think, I really don't think that anyone would really do a thing like that."
> "No?" the doctor said.
> "No. I can't really believe that anyone would do a thing of that sort intentionally." [4]

The doctor evades the complication by going for a walk.

In another instance, noted by Marcelline Hemingway Sanford, Dr. Hemingway reprimands Ernest for violating game laws, and when Ernest objects, saying, "Well, you do," he answers, "But I didn't get caught" [5]—a strange compromise for an uncompromising man. These incidents are of further interest because they are representative of the moral laxity of the early 1900's which continues to demoralize society today. Anything goes if you can get away with it. Hemingway's regret concerning this basic moral laxity is expressed in Lt. Henry's remorseful statement, "If only my father had taught me that you never get away with anything." [6] In *A Farewell to Arms* the end product of the good nights in Milan is the bad business of Catherine's death in the Lausanne hospital. In *Across the River and Into the Trees* Colonel Cantwell expresses this same regret, asking the shrimp, "O speedy shrimp, master of retreat, didn't they tell you the nets were dangerous?" [7]

(Ernest's mother, Grace Hall Hemingway, was Dr. Hemingway's opposite. She came from a family of money; he, from a family of poverty. She had been raised in the tradition of the arts, studying music and reading literature, painting and traveling, he in the tradition of the sciences, studying natural and physical sciences. She rebelled against the conventional restrictions placed on women in the 1880's and longed for freedom; he accepted convention and enjoyed discipline. She had an inner need to be alone and understood Ernest Hemingway's desire for solitude; Dr. Hemingway took this as a personal affront, and through the years the difference grew. Mrs. Hemingway said:

> I want the view from the top of the hill. It's worth going without water and food to have peace and quiet and to be alone. People are made differently. Some women cling to their husbands and their children. They want to possess them. Some women feed their egos by touching and owning members of their families. Others like to share their abilities and interests, but they need solitude and communication with God, the source. I must have quietness and peace to live. Ernest is very like me, and when he gets through this period of fighting himself and everyone else, he'll be a fine man.[8]

During Ernest's high-school years, Mrs. Hemingway was influential in having the children take dancing lessons in spite of Dr. Hemingway's repeated warning, "Leads to hell and damnation—don't know what this world's coming to—it's all your mother's idea—etc." Despite his father's restrictive religious discipline, Ernest remained devoted to the First Congregational Church. He and his sister even entered a Bible-reading contest, which proved to be beneficial to both. They were both active members of the League, and the record shows that Ernest often took charge of the Sunday-afternoon services.

Mrs. Hemingway and Dr. Hemingway continued to get on each other's nerves; and the minor difficulties that Marcelline Hemingway Sanford suggested were recorded as "hundreds of crises" in Leicester Hemingway's book, *My Brother, Ernest Hemingway*. As a girl of seven, Mrs. Hemingway had been left blind after an attack of scarlet fever (praying diligently, she had her sight restored). It has been suggested by Leices-

21

ter Hemingway that she would retire with sick headaches, using this as an escape from family problems, but her ability to adjust to bright light was seriously impaired and extreme light continued to cause her great pain throughout her life. In the short story "The Doctor and the Doctor's Wife," Ernest gives us a typical picture of his mother, who customarily sat in a darkened room for comfort.

Urged by his mother to accept responsibility and a job after World War I, Ernest grew more resentful of her influence and longed for his father's dominance. After his marriage to Hadley Richardson in a Methodist church at the cottage "Windemere," Walloon Lake, Michigan, Ernest accepted a job with the *Toronto Star*, which eventuated in the young couple's trip to Paris. They returned to the States temporarily for the birth of their son.[9] Ernest began to write seriously in an atmosphere of European culture, and friends such as Gertrude Stein proved to be influential. Family estrangement, due to the intensity of Ernest Hemingway's character, had already sent down its tap root, and upon the publication of his book *in our time*, it was firmly implanted. Ernest resented his father's hasty action of returning the books to the publisher. His correspondence with the family ceased, and it was only through the devoted effort of his wife Hadley that the grandparents were kept informed about their new grandson, John. Despite these differences, Ernest Hemingway clung to his original beliefs formed during his youth. Evidence supporting this statement is found in the report of Ernest and Ursala some forty years later in Havana, nostalgically recalling the visits of their Uncle Will, Dr. Hemingway's brother, who was a medical missionary to Shensi Province, China. They sang "Jesus Loves Me" in Chinese until the tears rolled down their cheeks.

The community into which Hemingway was born contributed also to his early religious development. Oak Park in 1900 boasted that it was the largest village in the United States. Along with this claim, Oak Park exhibited many of the traits typical of village life. The village was predominantly

22

Protestant middle class, and extremely provincial. Ernest's Oak Park existence was relatively sheltered. The town was righteously dry, and the center of the social life was the school and the family church. As evidenced in the conventional beliefs of Clarence Edmonds Hemingway, the puritanical influence did much to shape the accepted morality of the town. But it must not be assumed that the community is to blame for Ernest Hemingway's difficult adolescence. Two forces were at war in his being: the intensity of his own character and his highly competitive nature. Ernest tried to disguise his more somber aspect of life with a flippant buoyancy, but the Protestant metal had been cast, with only the test remaining. Forming Ernest's religious background were the tenets of the puritanical Congregational church, an austere belief colored by profound Episcopalian theology, which Ernest received from his Grandfather Hall and incorporated into most of his later writing.

CHAPTER II

THE 1920's: HEMINGWAY'S WAR EXPERIENCE AND THE DEVELOPMENT OF A MORAL CODE

A person cannot divorce his thinking from the tenor of the times. Whether Hemingway shared the beliefs of the disillusioned young generation of the postwar years and the later 1920's or not, his attitudes towards religion and morality were being formed by his experiences. Hemingway's character underwent a drastic transformation from the character of the nineteen-year-old Oak Park youth. Confronted with cruelty, as evidenced in war, he was put to the alternative of interposing to stop it or losing his sensibility. He chose a stoic façade as his weapon to shock his readers into the realizations he had faced. It is erroneous to assume that this facade was a part of his character, for it merely served as a guise to shelter a very sensitive nature.

Seymour Melman, in his recent book, *The Peace Race,* mentions four protective mechanisms one could assume to justify war: (1) the relative guiltlessness of the psychopathic personality, (2) the identification with moral aims that are socially approved, (3) the "obedient employee" (Eichmann), and (4) the dehumanized perception of inhuman effects.[1] It is obvious that Hemingway could not assume any of these protective mechanisms. Unlike the psychopath whose lack of moral responsibility permits him to commit inhuman acts without a sense of guilt, Hemingway felt a deep moral responsibility. Justification for killing, the killing of humans questioned in his war novels and the killing of animals questioned in *The Green Hills of Africa* and *The Old Man and the Sea,* became a main problem to him.

24

Ira Wolfert records that during the Turkish-Greco evacuation, Hemingway, overcome by emotion, said, "God, those small, white faces, like stepped-on flowers. They're so innocent, pure and forever throw away." [2] Hemingway, like Camus, struggled against a universe where children suffer and die. Hemingway's characters testify to this tragic feeling of waste in many of the views they express. Richard Cantwell, in *Across the River and Into the Trees,* can't seem to justify his wrong decisions. He says, "You were right ninety-five per cent of the time, but how do you explain away the five per cent of the time you were wrong?" [3] Learning to live with his moral mistakes was a difficult task resulting in overabundant bitterness. Anselmo, in *For Whom the Bell Tolls,* can find justification and satisfaction in a bear's paw nailed to the door of the church as a trophy of the kill, but questions the morality of the man's hand nailed in its place. The Christian reference to the nailed hand of Christ comes to mind. Hemingway's question is aimed at the very core of Christian belief. The acceptance of the death of Christ as a sacrifice is an acceptance of the unjust killing of an innocent man. The fifth commandment, "Thou shalt not kill," is foremost in Jordan's and Anselmo's discussion of the sin of killing. In the little play, "Today Is Friday," the question of the morality of killing arises again. The three soldiers represent three different moralities: one is a skeptic, the other feels that the suffering is admirable, and the third is filled with nausea.[4] These examples give evidence that Hemingway and his characters recognize killing as bizarre and exceptional in human conduct.

In hunting game and in fishing Hemingway is also concerned about the justification of killing. He questions in *Green Hills of Africa* whether he is being punished for killing animals, as he recalls a painfully shattered arm he was made to endure. He speaks of feeling sick when he wounded a bull sable, and remarks, "Even killing a buffalo, you feel a little quiet inside." [5] "If one must kill, it should be clean and quick." [6] Finally, he comes to the conclusion, "after taking a long time to make up his mind," that "it is a sin to kill any nondangerous game animal except for meat." [7] A Hemingway character, Santiago, in *The Old Man and the Sea,* considers the possibility that killing the fish was a sin. He seems to be obsessed by the idea, repeating, "You killed him for pride because you are a fisherman. You loved him when he was alive and you loved him after. If you love him, it is not a sin to kill him. Or is it more? You think too much, old man." [8]

The Hemingway of the early 1920's would find it impossible to identify himself with moral aims which were socially approved. World War I had been a war to "end all wars." Wilson called it a "crusade for freedom." Promises were made that "these dead shall not have died in vain, and we must fight to make the world safe for democracy." This war, fought on a highly idealistic plane, rang hollow tones in the sensitive soul of Ernest Hemingway. He summarizes his beliefs in *A Farewell to Arms,* when Lt. Henry says:

> I was always embarrassed by the words sacred, glorious, and sacrifice and the expression in vain. We had heard them, sometimes standing in the rain almost out of earshot, so that only the shouted words came through, and had read them on proclamations that were slapped up by bill-posters over other proclamations now for a long time, and I had seen nothing sacred, and the things that were glorious had no glory and the sacrifices were like the stockyard of Chicago if nothing was done with the meat except bury it. There were many words that you could not stand to hear and finally only the names of places had dignity. Abstract words such as glory, honor, courage, or hallow were obscene beside the concrete names of villages, the numbers of roads, the names of rivers, the numbers of regiments and dates. [9]

He frequently reacted against the "holy abstractions" of Western civilization, which, in the midst of trench warfare and melancholy retreats, seemed a culmination of profanity against the dignity of man. Hemingway cannot claim to be unique in his conviction, but he is extremely forceful. Conventional abstractionism is disastrous when translated into rules for conduct in action. The moral code achieved is that of the double standard, and man is given the right to shoot another man in the idealism of war.[10] Hemingway had had enough of high causes and noble sacrifices. He was ready to make "a separate peace." His rejection of society's aims is repeated throughout *in our time* and *A Farewell to Arms.* The very title of the latter rings a note of finality to his moral decision.

Hemingway in a later period came close to accepting Melman's third alternative, the "obedient employee": a belief which he explored in the novels *For Whom the Bell Tolls* and *Across the River and Into the Trees.* Robert Jordan exhibits an extreme sense of duty in his mission to blow up the bridge, and admits that if he is to maintain this sense of proportion he cannot permit himself to think; to aid his non-thinking state, Jordan drinks absinthe, a habit-forming liquor.

A counterpoint to the earlier passage in *A Farewell to Arms* is the following passage in *For Whom the Bell Tolls,* which further stresses Jordan's sense of duty. One will note a slight change in his character's feeling towards "holy abstractions":

> At either of those places you felt that you were taking part in a crusade. That was the only word for it although it was a word that had been so worn and abused that it no longer gave its true meaning. You felt, in spite of all bureaucracy and inefficiency and party strife something that was like the feeling you expected to have after your first communion. It was a feeling of consecration to a duty toward all of the oppressed of the world which would be difficult and embarrassing to talk about as a religious experience and yet it was as authentic as when you heard Bach, or stood in Chartres Cathedral or the Cathedral at Leon and saw the lights coming through the great windows, or when you saw Montegna, Greco, Brueghel in Prado. It gave you a part of something you could believe in wholly, completely, and an absolute brotherhood.[11]

The apocalypse of history in the classless society is no more justified than the coming of the Kingdom of Heaven. In both of these faiths the injustices and evils of this life are transformed into temporary goods in the light of the apocalypse. It is the promise and the certainty of the ultimate justification of the cause which make it possible for men to give themselves willingly as a sacrifice for this cause. When the ultimate values of human existence lie beyond and at the end of history, men can die meaningfully. Justification of their sacrifice will come only at the end of time. If the justification does not lie in the future it will remain an injustice and the sacrifices meaningless. Likewise, Jordan's rationalization falls short of ideal sacrifice. Creeping into his thinking is the belief of Anselmo, the Christian who is perplexed by the problem of forgiveness in a Republic that had given up God. Jordan recalls another Christian's accounts of an American Civil War, with its unjustifiable numbers of sick and dying, and justification of duty seems absurd.

Richard Cantwell, likewise a professional soldier, considers his duty but concludes, "I can't hate anyone." He is a bitter old soldier who cannot purge himself of guilt and whose conscience will not permit him to sleep. Renata falls asleep as he is relating his war experiences; and he, as Brutus to his boy Lucius, says, "Sleep on, my beauty." Youth is not troubled by such moral issues. Richard Cantwell and Robert Jordan suffer the mental anguish which Shakespeare's Brutus suffered trying to justify his moral position of duty to the Republic of Rome. All sacrificed their lives because of their belief. It may be significant to remember that while Jesus, who also sacrificed his life for his belief, was in the Garden of Gethsemane, the disciples slept and Jesus returned, saying, "What—could ye not watch with me one hour?" [12]

Hemingway explored the last psychological device, which was to perceive in a dehumanized way the inhuman effects of war. All feelings were to be excluded and human consequences selectively ignored. To achieve this it is necessary to stress the technical aspects of war, reasoning on a formal plane. Hemingway satirizes this solution in the chapters in *in our time,* in which human life is pictured at its lowest worth. The intended question arises whether we as humans can accept a purely psychological answer. Will we treat with a cool intellect the annihilation of a certain percentage of people as if they were pawns in a game of chess? Army Intelligence always plans to lose a number of men. The question becomes—rather, how many can they afford to lose?

Edmund Wilson recognized these same moral values being questioned in the vignettes and in the emergence of the rudimentary values of Nick Adams, which later form the basis for the Hemingway moral code.[13] Robert Jordan attempts to dehumanize his mission to dynamite and strategy, but the inescapable human element destroys his reasoning. Anselmo, Maria and even the traitor Pablo bring back childhood scenes of persecution of one's brother. Jordan recalls the ugliness of an American society which permitted a Negro to be hanged from a lamp post and burned, and remembers a general who was drunk during most of a civil war. Man's inhumanity to man looms large to Robert Jordan. "These Spaniards are brothers, not enemies," he says. Richard Cantwell says, "It sure seemed strange to see a German dog eat a baked German. You wouldn't think that could be possible." He adds, "These are not my enemies." [14] In the famous account of the retreat from Caporetto, Lt. Henry tells of the inhumanity of war, exemplified by the Italians unknowingly killing their own men. Santiago, in *The Old Man and the Sea,* says it isn't right to live on the sea and kill your brother. The irony of the conclusion is expressed in Jordan's comment, "The church said not to think about it and that's pretty advice." [15]

Hemingway, in all of the above examples, despite a slight wavering, has solved that portion of his moral code which recognizes war as totally immoral and unjustifiable. He has progressed from the shocked recoil of his youthful experience to his fight with mankind, using bitter satire as an effective weapon, and in his later years to his acceptance of moral responsibility to mankind, his brother. Hemingway must now face the reality of life without the compulsion to run away or to satirize his resentment.

This statement, in the preface to the book *Men at War,* sums up the feeling he has revealed through his characters:

> I hate war and all politicians whose mismanagement, gullibility, cupidity, selfishness, and ambition brought on the War of 1916-17. When you go to war as a boy you have a great illusion of immortality. Other people get killed, not you. It can happen to other people, but not you. Then when you were badly wounded the first time you lose that illusion and you know it can happen to you. After being severely wounded two weeks before my nineteenth birthday I had a bad time until I figured it out that nothing could happen to me that had not happened to all men before me. Whatever I had to do men had always done. If they had done it I could do it too. The best thing was not to worry about it. "By my troth, I care not, a man can die but once; we owe God a death and let it go which way it will, he that dies this year is quit the next." [16]

It is obvious that Hemingway continues to place the blame on individuals and avoids the conception of original sin. He refuses to accept the theory of the complacent Christians that this life is only a vale of tears in which happiness is out of place, since we are all guilty. As a young boy, he believed, as Edna St. Vincent Millay believed, that "Childhood is a kingdom where nobody dies"; but as a result of the war he realized that he was not immortal, and in the face of death his moral code needed strengthening.

Hemingway's morality had reached the stage where he questioned what is acceptable and what is not acceptable. His brother Leicester Hemingway attests to Ernest's strong moral position, saying, "Should Ernest decide to forgive, the recipient might spend the rest of his life in gratitude at being freed from his version of Coventry." [17] Hemingway questions what is immortal and suggests through the love affair of Jordan and Maria that love is the only immortal experience capable of creating a oneness of mankind. All activities of mankind lead to death, but love alone stands triumphant over death. This premise, carried a little further, would state that this kind of love, like the love of God who so loved the world that he gave his only begotten son to die, is man's only hope.

Hemingway may or may not have accepted this conclusion. He humbly sought to know why he believed what he believed. He was not dependent upon the statement of moral principle, but dependent upon experience to develop this for him. In *Death in the Afternoon* Hemingway states his moral position of knowing right from wrong when he says, "All I know is that what is moral is what you feel good after and what is immoral is what you feel bad after." [18] Continuing, he says, "The bullfight is moral to me because I feel fine while it is going on and have a feeling of life and death, mortality and immortality, and after it is over I feel sad but fine."

A similar result is achieved by true tragedy in the ancient tradition of Aristotle. One undergoes a catharsis, or purging, of evil emotions while witnessing a tragedy. Hemingway's emphatic response to the noble death of the bull likewise purges his emotions. In *The Sun Also Rises* Jake echoes the phrase, "Immorality is things that made you disgusted afterwards." Richard Cantwell, in *Across the River and Into the Trees,* does not feel good after he calls Renata. Contrary to the critics' belief that this is immature, the code, applied truthfully, is extremely rigid. His code of ethics is as rigid as any found in any religion. There could be no gray areas between right and wrong. Naked truth becomes the only formula to use in achieving morality. There is no twilight. It is either day or night, either yes or no, good or evil, salvation or damnation: as stated in Romans 2:15, "The law is written in their hearts, their conscience also, bearing witness."

Behind the appetite of the physical world lies the tragedy and falsity of moral relations. Hemingway's hatred of sham and posturing occupies a good portion of his writing. His sly blow

31

at the religion of his day is his pointed comment, "Anselmo was a Christian, which is something rare in Catholic countries." This could be expanded to say that Grandfather Hall was a Christian, which is something rare in Protestant countries. Hemingway was sickened by sentimentalized religion and sentimentalized faith. Christians whining and whimpering their prayers to an Almighty God were intolerable, to his thinking. Through their blind, sickly stupor he felt they were sending their souls to hell. Fear and weakness were the neurosis from which their religion suffered.

Hemingway's conception of the Christian façade is very similar to that of Camus, and Father Festugière who said:

> Some people may have religious faith, may practice that faith outwardly without experiencing the anguish of religious problems. They attend mass, take communion at Easter, fulfill varied obligations of Christian law through a feeling of tradition or through the simple desire to fulfill what is due in respect to the divine, or even to liberate themselves from some disquietude once and for all through observing the rites instituted by men for that purpose, so that, having observed them, they may no longer have to think about them. Conversely, one may adhere to no creed whatever, perform no religious practices, yet be tortured throughout one's life by the problem of God, of what He is, of the relations between God and man.[19]

Hemingway's attitude would not have been as pagan as the converse section of the above quotation, for we have evidence that he not only respects but partially accepts the beliefs of true Christians. Hemingway's respect of the true, dedicated Christian, whether Protestant or Catholic, is shown in all his writing. Lt. Henry respects the priest, who has a dry, clean mind. Mr. Frazer respects the nun who desired to become a saint. Robert Jordan respects Anselmo, a Christian. Jake says, in reply to Brett's comment that this is what we

32

have instead of God, "Many have God." Ernest Hemingway respects his Grandfather Hall, another Christian.

Hemingway's attitude towards sham and hypocrisy is summed up in Emily Dickinson's poem:

> I like a look of agony
> Because I know it's true;
> Men do not sham convulsion
> Nor simulate a throe.
> The eyes glaze once and that is death,
> Impossible to feign,
> The beads upon the forehead
> By homely anguish strung.[20]

Hemingway's search for the truth in life led him to become closely associated with death and suffering.

Hemingway, as well as his contemporaries, despaired of the corruption of the times, for corruption had seeped into religions as well as society. Truth was at a premium. Anselmo, in *For Whom the Bell Tolls,* said that the churches were full of sin, and his comment that they did not have God any more could be interpreted to mean that though the edifice still stands, the Church is dead. During the Spanish Civil War of 1937, Hemingway's strong Loyalist belief paralleled that of his character Anselmo, causing many family arguments with his pro-Catholic second wife, Pauline Pfeiffer. Her loyalty lay with the corrupt Spanish church, which clung to the ancient Inquisition.

With this same fiery blast, Hemingway attacks American Protestantism. Returning home after his war experience, he found his boyhood ideals shattered and his thinking crystalizing. Krebs, in "Soldier's Home," may be this young Hemingway incapable of adjusting to a predominantly provincial Protestant middle-class society. "Soldier's Home" might mean, satirically, a place of retirement for a complete war hazard. In this story of fitting and non-fitting, Krebs cannot mold his altered beliefs into the pattern of the past. The middle-class sentimentalism and moralism lacked significant religious depth, because they forfeited immediacy of relation both with God and with nature. D. H. Lawrence speaks in writing about hymns of "The ghastly sentimentalism that came like a leprosy over religion." [21] Reality of Christian worship cannot be restored by injections of saccharine.

After the war, people in Europe seemed more real to Hemingway than did the people in America, because the Europeans knew suffering and death on a much larger scale and had been forced to face reality.[22] A breakdown of the moral code was one of the frantic results of the war. The American people reacted to this breakdown through Prohibition, a violent puritanical attempt to stem the tide of moral laxity. Hemingway rebelled against the narrow view which the Puritans held in regard to many social restraints. Two of his stories attacked the puritanical sexual code. In "God Rest Ye, Merry Gentlemen," a youth is troubled by his natural desires, which he assumes are bad, and mutilates himself because of his inhibitory puritanical belief. In the story "Mr. and Mrs. Eliot," the husband is restrained in his sexual relation with his wife. Hemingway seems to be suggesting here that Puritan granite can either strengthen or crush.

Religion had become mixed with human morality, and true faith had become engulfed in a stream of man-made restrictions. Petty Victorian concern centered around the morality of dancing, drinking and card-playing, while the truly immoral issues, such as war, were permitted to masquerade under banners. Repeatedly in his writing Hemingway refers to dead religions. In "The Gambler, the Nun, and the Radio," Mr. Frazer calls religion an opium of the people. People had evolved into "form Christians." In the *Green Hills of Africa,* Hemingway says that religion is a joke for the people who have it, or something which is not done seriously. Lt. Henry, in *A Farewell to Arms,* says he has no religion, but the man still prays and accepts God.

Hemingway's criticism of the religions of his day does not verify his disbelief, as so many critics have erroneously assumed, but rather verifies that he had a hard time justifying his belief within the structure of any particular religion. Although Hemingway was rebellious towards some of the more recently developed restraints which claimed puritanical heritage, he found Mencken, one of American's greatest enemies of Puritanism, impossible to read and, one might add, to accept. In *The Sun Also Rises,* the conversation between Jake and Harvey reveals this conclusion:

> "Do you know Mencken, Harvey?"
>
> "Yes, why?"
>
> "What's he like?"
>
> "He's all right. He says some pretty funny things. Last time I had dinner with him we talked about Hoffenheimer. 'The trouble is,' he said, 'he's a garter snapper!' That's not bad."
>
> "That's not bad."
>
> "He's through now." Harvey went on, "He's written about all the things he knows and now he's on all the things he doesn't know."
>
> "I guess he's all right," I said. "I just can't read him."
>
> "Oh, nobody reads him now," Harvey said, "except the people that used to read the Alexander Hamilton Institute."
>
> "Well," I said, "that was a good thing too." [23]

Hemingway cannot seem to escape his Protestant puritanical tradition, and is out of tune with many in the 1920's when he exhibits such virtues as discipline in place of uncontrolled liberty, industry in place of aimless pleasure-seeking, thrift in place of extravagance, and truth in place of evasion.

Ernest Hemingway questioned whether American Protestantism, strongly puritanical and provincial, had become one and the same thing: an anemic offshoot of an ancient belief. Had the churches lost their awareness of the fateful issue of good and evil? Had Protestantism become the law of man designed to overthrow the law of God? What was the moral code God intended man to follow? Hemingway was to devote his entire career trying to find God's intent for his gift of life.

As pointed out in Chapter I, in the story "The Doctor and the Doctor's Wife," the doctor is incapable of standing firm on the moral issue of stealing. The wife offers the balm of a twisted Bible passage to help the doctor decide what was right and what was wrong. It is meant as a "cure all," as the wife is, significantly, a Christian Scientist, with her *Quarterly Science and Health With a Key to the Scriptures* by her side. The scripture was supposed to support the doctor's position. Use was being made of the scriptures to justify a moral position rather than use of the scriptures to find the truth. The doctor is falling into the pitfall of modern morality: anything is all right if you can get away with it. This revolution in morals had begun as a middle-class children's revolt, resolving itself in a belief of being found out. The middle class had also begun to misinterpret the meaning of the word "prosper" as to grow wealthy. Materialism was steadily affecting the moral fiber of the generation. This decaying moral code was encouraged rather than discouraged under the protective hand of a religion which refused to see life as it actually was. What ailed America was a Puritan mind and a Calvinist tradition of repression. Pseudo-idealistic American Protestantism had become a dead religion.

F. Scott Fitzgerald gives statement to this belief, saying, "We returned to find all Gods dead, all wars fought, all faiths in man shaken." [24] Hemingway, too, suffered the disillusion Fitzgerald so aptly stated. Hemingway's disgust is not so much a disgust with American Protestantism as it was conceived but rather as it had become: the law of man enforced with misread proof from the scriptures. Religion had become a paint to gloss a rotting structure.

Hemingway has often been called an escapist, but this is a false accusation, for he ridicules society for being escapist, using idealism to escape from life as it actually existed: to escape from faith as it was written. His plea is, "Be true." Ad-

36

mittedly, there are times when Hemingway cannot accept society, but his separate peace is more representative of an individual's right of opinion than of an individual's renouncing society. Hemingway's compassion for his fellow man places him *"in medias res."*

At no time in his writing does Hemingway stand apart from life as a pedant, but rather he is involved in a mutual struggle to determine good and evil. His purpose is not didactic in a positive sense, but in a negative sense.

In "A Clean Well-Lighted Place" an old man who had attempted suicide sits searching for truth, which is represented by the light. He is obsessed by death, by a meaningless world, by nothingness. His despair is that felt by a man who hungers for a sense of order and assurance that others seem to put in religious faith, but who cannot find grounds for his own faith. The waiter, attempting to pray the "Our Father" and "Hail Mary," finds the words mean nothing without the "light" and a "certain cleanness and order." He concludes praying, "Our nada, who art in nada—Hail nothing, full of nothing." Words mean nothing without the "light" which is symbolic of truth. The prayers are empty and hollow. That life is vain is re-echoed from Ecclesiastes, but from the ruins comes another echo, of man's preparation for a renaissance beyond the limits of nihilism. Similarly, in the story "The Gambler, the Nun, and the Radio," Mr. Frazer shows a profound respect for the nun, who has God and truth, but continues to believe that the radio has become an opium of the people. The habit of not thinking is the vice that has hidden true faith. The only truth is knowledge: clean and dry. This knowledge is God brought about by revolution, which is not an opium.

These two stories, mentioned above, are similar in the religious belief being presented. In "A Clean Well-Lighted Palace," to take one's life is an act of cowardice and an act of bad faith. Life is absurd, but to live is to make the absurd live. To make it live is to face it squarely. Continuing this reasoning, in the light of the second story, "The Gambler, the Nun, and the Radio," revolt becomes the answer: one transcends absurdity by protesting. Everything has become absurd except knowledge, which can be had through revolution.

Amidst the 1920's World Series type of atmosphere, with undue concern over things which seemed exciting but not too important, religious skepticism flourished in the minds of thinking men. In a news release, Hemingway describes the people's desire that Paris be a "super-Sodom and a grander-Gomorrah." Old Testament decadence is brought back into our consciences. Science was debunking old-time religion, and with the advance of hedonism church attendance began to drop off. Hemingway rigidly upheld true skepticism as basic to all truth. He says about bullfighters that, "at the start of their careers all are as devoutly ritualistic as altar boys serving a high Mass and some always remain so. Others are as cynical as nightclub proprietors. The devout ones are killed more frequently. The cynical ones are the best companions. But the best of all are the cynical ones when they are still devout; or after; when having been devout, then cynical, they become devout again by cynicism." [25] Skepticism can be deeply religious in quality, for, "Whatsoever a generation soweth that shall it reap." Skepticism is saved from becoming agnosticism because it leaves the heart open to hope and faith. As the good Christian in St. Mark's gospel, Hemingway's ideal Christian would say, "Lord, I believe, help thou my unbelief."

Hemingway's *The Sun Also Rises* is an excellent example of a cynical satire written about Paris in the 1920's. It was patterned after the Biblical satire, called Ecclesiastes, meaning "preacher." A brief account of the book in the Bible would probably be as follows: (1) Introduction: Everything is vain, for man, during his life on earth, is more transient than nature, whose unchangeable course he admires but does not comprehend. "The sun also rises and the sun goeth down but the earth abideth forever." (2) Part I: "All things are vain, including wisdom, pleasures, pomp and, therefore, is it not better to enjoy life's blessings which God has given than to waste your strength uselessly?" The epilogue to this part is added proof that all things are immutably predestined and are not subject to man's will. Self-accusation, because of excessive luxury, is placed in the foreground. (3) Part II: Life is vain and cheerless, because of the iniquity in the courts of justice. Mad competition leads many to fall into idleness. A serious life free from frivolity is best. Instead of passionate outbreaks, Qoheleth recommends a golden mean. Finally, he inquires into the deepest and last reason of "vanity" and finds it in the will of God that Misery entered the world. His admonition is to enjoy in peace and modesty the blessings granted by God, instead of giving oneself up to anger, on account of wrongs endured, or to avarice or other vices.[26]

Hemingway's theme in *The Sun Also Rises* parallels this story of Ecclesiastes. It, too, is a sombre book with a negative lesson. Its story repeats the warning that sloth destroys nations. One must work diligently and win but leave the success to God—a conclusion repeated in Hemingway's short-story collection, *Winner Take Nothing*. Hemingway firmly believed that a person never really has anything until he gives it away. Jake, exemplifying the above belief, is not like the others, for he must work and live a disciplined life. Even amid pleasures, he is called back to God and repents that he is not a better Catholic. Jake, a fatalistic pessimist, recognizes the freedom of man. Despite his negative attitude, he is capable of showing the deepest sympathy for the misery and suffering of mankind. He pities Brett and all those who cannot control their lives. He recognizes the evils of the world and is impressed by them, such as the sinfulness of women, which causes the trouble at the Pamplona festival. The colors Hemingway uses to paint these evils observed by Jake are every bit as daring as the colors of Qoheleth.

Hemingway is wrestling with the riddle of life: man's true happiness must not be looked for on earth, not in human wisdom, not in luxury, and not in royal splendor. Many afflictions await everybody as a consequence of their own passions. Brett is ruled and ruined by her passions. Yet God does not deny a person a small measure of happiness if he does not seek beyond or above that intended for mankind.

Brett's unrest led her beyond her intended station in life. Cohn, with his spaniel fawning, was no longer a man, but he fortunately realized his mistake in time to gain back some of the happiness allotted to him. Michael, an aristocrat ruined by excessive luxury, would continue drinking down the path of destruction. Jake alone could view the scene objectively and have pity for each in his turn. Throughout life, Hemingway, like his character Jake, exhibits Christian forgiveness and pity, with the conviction that "There but for the grace of God, go I."

Ernest Hemingway's *The Sun Also Rises* is one of the books which Halford Luccock suggests hold strong claim to a Pulitzer Prize for Christian Evangelism (if such an award were given).[27] Utter absence of religion or idealism in *The Sun Also Rises* is matched by an utter absence of happiness or the reflection of it.

Marian Sanders, in a satirical comment in Luccock's book, stated that *"The Sun Also Rises* is the great moral tract of the age. It will drive all the amateur reprobates in the English-speaking world to the cold showers. Mr. Hemingway has painted the most unalluring picture of vice yet achieved by mortal pen." She feels that his negative lesson was unintended. The negative intended testimony to the necessity of a spiritual content to life is just as persuasive as positive assertion. Its additional worth lies in the force it carries in many quarters where the more positive form of assertion would be dismissed as moralistic preaching. His novel demonstrates that more freedom is in itself an empty gain, for many confuse freedom with license. When license becomes the liberty for anybody to do anything at any time, freedom from want becomes freedom from work; freedom of worship, freedom from worship; freedom of speech, freedom from truth; freedom from fear, freedom from duty. Repeated in his later writing, this theme of destruction resulting because a man goes out too far is developed in the old fisherman Santiago.

Another repeated theme in *The Sun Also Rises*[28] is the constancy of the land, which is, likewise, found in the *Green*

Hills of Africa. Hemingway says, "I had loved country all my life; the country was always better than the people. I could only care about people a very few at a time." [29]

This same intense feeling can be felt in the fresh descriptions of Spanish mountains, upland valleys and streams in *For Whom the Bell Tolls.* Nick Adams' benediction to the land in "The Big Two-Hearted River" echoes the refrain: "It is good." Man needs to be rooted to the soil to attain full vitality. The profound relation of man, a creator, the primordial medium of his spiritual life, and the ancient bond to the earth affords a natural religion.

Charles Roven claims that "The basic element in religion is the sense of reality that is outside ourselves and is not relative but absolute, of values which carry compelling assent of something fixed and eternal, abiding while all else may change and giving to the transient its worth." [30] To Hemingway, the earth is absolute and gives value to the transient.

The greatness of land and transient man humbled before its might became the subject of Ernest Hemingway. Sherwood Anderson before him, sounding the depths of common experience with tenderness, had as his subject the aimless, perpetual-searching man who reached complete humility. Randall Stewart has said, "If our democracy is to survive and thrive, it will be necessary that a genuine Christian humility become an important part of our consciences." [31] This genuine Christian humility became a part of the consciences of Ernest Hemingway and Sherwood Anderson: man was humbled before a mighty universe. Hemingway's version assumes a sense of universality, expanding to include the suffering and unhappiness of all mankind. Men, in a never-ending stream, have gone to search out the high places of the earth and have lifted their eyes to view the face of God. Upon the slopes, they are challenged by danger, privation and adventure, all ending in suffering which results in pure humility.

Hemingway constantly speaks of pain and suffering as humiliating and something that men have to endure. On the contrary, the assumption of our materialistic culture is that we have the right to comfort and ease and should avoid suffering. Elizabeth Barrett Browning said, "But knowledge by suffering endureth." Perhaps in seeking comfort and avoiding pain we are getting off the evolutionary path. Paradoxically, suffering is most poignantly felt when physical comforts are in abundance. Close the door of the body to suffering and it will come through the mind. [32]

Central to Christian faith is the suffering of Christ. How did Christ endure pain? Hemingway asks this question in "Today Is Friday." He answers, "He was pretty good in there today." He humbled himself, even to the death of the cross. In Spain, pain was something to be endured.[33] The good that are humble die soon, but God keeps the bad around until he reminds them that too much honor kills a man. In "A Dangerous Summer," Antonio is said to have the pride of the devil, and pride and vainglory are the products of the devil. Hemingway recognizes the love of killing and believes that taking on godlike attributes of giving death is an act of pride, a Christian sin and a pagan virtue.

Hemingway's life was always a testimony of Philippians 2:3, "Let nothing be done through strife or vainglory but in lowliness of mind, let each esteem others better than themselves." Hemingway says, "If people bring so much courage to this world, the world has to kill them to break them, so, of course, it kills them. The world breaks every one, and afterward many are strong at the broken places. But those who will not break are killed. It kills the very good, gentle, and brave impartially. If you are none of these you can be sure it will kill you, but there is no hurry." [34]

The other great sin, according to Hemingway, was self-righteousness. In *Green Hills of Africa* he says, "I hated any one who was righteous over pain, or who was righteous at all, or who had ever been righteous. I hated all righteous bastards." [35]

In Hemingway's novels man is humbled before this mighty universe. Lt. Henry is made to suffer through the death of his son and Catherine. Robert Jordan suffers because of his belief and dies humbly beneath the mighty pines, with the needle-covered floor as his crucifixion bier. Santiago cries in anguish as Our Lord, "Ayee, Ayee," completely humbled. Harry Morgan is humbled beneath the majestic heights of Kilimanjaro and repents the loss of his talent and so little time left to recover it. Another Harry Morgan, in *To Have and Have Not,* suffers and is reduced to humility and death on the boat he has used to transport a group of revolutionist robbers. He says, "A man has no chance alone." He needs help, whether it is the help of man or God. Richard Cantwell, an old army general, has a hand like Christ to testify to his crucifixion by the world. Not only his hand but his death, also, parallel that of Our Lord.

Sidney Lanier's poem, "The Ballad of the Trees and the Master," begins, "Into the woods my Master went . . ." Richard Cantwell also went into the woods to rest a while. The impotent Jake Barnes suffers from a love which he cannot fulfill in that modern Sodom and Gomorrah—Paris, 1920. Nick Adams suffers the shock of World War I.

In Hemingway's short stories, likewise, the element of humiliating pain is constantly present. The echo, "Ayee, Ayee," of Santiago resounds through "The Natural History of the Dead" and "The Snows of Kilimanjaro" as the cry of the dying Christ on the cross, "Eloi Eloi, lama Sabachtani," a moment of doubt in the passion of life.

Throughout all this pain and suffering, there exist faith and affirmation. Those of us who are willing to struggle, to suffer greatly for wholly ideal ends, will recognize the high road as the good road. In "A Clean Well-Lighted Place," the "light" or knowledge of God is high and the spotted or "unclean" bar is low. With all knowledge and pride, one needs to know nothing and feel nothing to come to complete humility. Security is not the whole of life, and a final lesson to be learned from Santiago, Wilson and Harry Morgan is that there are other conquests to be won than those over our fellow man.

But the major lesson to be learned from man's adventures on the mountain is that a man is never so much so as when he is striving to reach beyond his grasp. The only battle worth winning is that over ignorance and fear. It is not the goal which counts, but the struggle for it. There can be no Christian faith without the struggle, no true human sympathy without it. Our dilemma, then, is how through disciplined living we may come to terms with our own suffering and share the pain of others to compromise the world's tragedy.

Carlos Baker has shown that the mountains in Hemingway's novels serve not only as a symbol of man's humiliation but also as man's search for an eternal faith. In *A Farewell to Arms,* the mountains stand beckoning Lt. Henry to search for the ultimate wisdom, but he procrastinates. In *The Sun Also Rises,* the fishing experience in the mountains is clean and good. In *For Whom the Bell Tolls,* Robert Jordan dies in the mountains. In *The Old Man and the Sea,* Santiago struggles up the hill with his mast held in a crosslike position. *Across the River and Into the Trees* is set against a background of mountains. *Green Hills of Africa* is a story of pursuit in the hills. In "The Snows of Kilimanjaro," Harry Morgan is haunted by the thought that he will not have time to reclaim a lost talent but will be found crucified on the slopes, as the leopard is crucified. It is interesting to note that Douglas Hall Orrok says that "The African belief is in the external soul, which supposes a blood kinship between the leopard as the Doppelganger of the man, Harry, near the west peak of Kilimanjaro." [36]

The shadow of the mountain falls on all, humiliating man before its majesty. Each man must meet the struggle on the mountain. Nick Adams noted that nothing could happen to him that had not happened to all men before him. "If they had done it, I could do it too." Nick Adams and Hemingway are one and the same man in this belief, because Hemingway says the same thing in his introduction to *Men at War*. Hemingway continued his questioning, "How had it been for others?"

From the shepherd boy David, who used his sling on a scrubby hillside, through the crusade of St. Louis IX, to the present day, Hemingway reviewed man's suffering on the mountains that reduced him to abject humility and death.

Hemingway personally loved mountains, whether they were the mountains of Spain, Italy, Switzerland, Africa or Idaho. In the mountains he could purify and recreate himself in silence. Significantly, Jesus often went into the mountains and taught some of his greatest lessons from them. In the Old Testament, Moses received the Ten Commandments in the mountains. From time immemorial the mountains have been designated as a place where man could communicate with God.

Hemingway definitely felt that we could, with a certain degree of luck, live out life as God intended it. He explored God's intent for mankind in all his writing. Every atom in the universe is a part of a larger plan, and man's actions and deeds will contribute to, or detract from, the end result. Hemingway sought to realize the vast harmonious pattern of nature and the miraculous simplicity of the whole in a world darkened by hatred, srife, fear and doubt. Hemingway once said, "See that pelican in the sky—I don't know yet what his part is in the scheme of things."[37] He knew it factually, but he meant that it all had to become so deeply familiar that you knew it emotionally, as if by instinct, and that only came after a long time, through long, unconscious reflection. And it could be added, as Hemingway believed that all men must suffer and no man has the right to whine in life. To avoid domination of death makes for messiness in life which is a form of cheating.

A fitting conclusion is Hemingway's theme in *For Whom the Bell Tolls,* from John Donne:

No man is an iland intire of it selfe; every man is a piece of the Continent, a part of the maine: if a Clod bee washed away by the Sea, Europe is the lesse as well as if a Promontorie were, as well as if a Mannor of thy friends or

45

of thine owne were; any man's death diminishes me, because I am involved in Mankinde; And therefore never send to know for whom the bell tolls; It tolls for thee.

This then is the challenge—to live life so that, in the end, one faces death with courage. As in a game, disobedience to the rules results in a messy death. However, if man plays the game with courage and a certain degree of honor, he is rewarded a noble death. A bullfighter faces death admirably.

Throughout Hemingway's novels, man, acting in co-ordination with the will of God, is responsible unto death. He states in *Green Hills of Africa,* "Every damned thing is your fault if you're any good." Disobedience to the will of God ends in ignominious death. Retributive justice was to concern Hemingway in much of his writing. As a young boy, his character Nick Adams found his prayers sticking on the phrase directly preceding "Thy will be done." [38] This immature reaction to the will of God is further stressed by the memory of the childhood prayer, "Now I lay me . . ."

Sheridan Baker suggests that the childhood prayers may be a form of humility. He probably based his reasoning on the Bible passage, "Unless you come as a child you cannot enter the kingdom of Heaven." Lt. Henry, though basically immature, is haunted by the problem of retributive justice. If Lt. Frederick Henry truly loved God, he would not sin against Him and, having sinned against Him, he fears Him. In speaking to Greffi, he says that he does not love God but he fears Him at night. "The priest had always known what I did not know and what, when I learned it, I was able to forget. I did not know that then, although I learned it later." The religious note sounded is: "Love and sin no more. Respect the will of God."

Lt. Henry bargains with God, saying, "You do this for me and I'll do something for you," but begins to question whether he is deserving of God's consideration. He speaks of Catherine's delivery as an "Inquisition," placing her on trial. He also refers to the delivery as "the mill-race" (the mills of God). He asks

46

the waiter for some veal, and the waiter answers, "It is finished." Many hundreds of years before, Our Savior repeated these words, giving up the Holy Ghost, dying for the sins of the world. And now again, it is finished; Catherine will die because they sinned. Lt. Henry eats slowly and goes to pay his "reckoning," which could be interpreted to mean that this is his punishment.[39] Catherine says, "Death is just a dirty trick." Hemingway refers to the death of the obscene hyena as a "dirty joke," also in *Green Hills of Africa*. The love appetite of Catherine is comparable to the hideous "appetite" of the cowardly, but strong, hyena.

This is not the "Romeo and Juliet" type of love affair it has often been called. Innocence plays no part in their love. Romeo and Juliet have one night, their marriage night, together; and then to save this perfect love before it is marred by the sins of the world, Shakespeare completes his story and has the reader experience the tragic waste of these two lovers through their untimely death. It is an injustice to pure love to parallel the affair of Lt. Henry and Catherine with youthful innocence. Tragic, yes—but Lt. Henry had learned to love Catherine in spite of resistance. Catherine ignores marriage vows and remains sinful without repentance to the last. She approaches death with pride, mistaken for courage, rather than with the necessary humility of a truly noble death—or, as Hemingway calls it, "a clean joke," in talking about the death of birds in *Green Hills of Africa,* or death faced in a pure way, in *Death in the Afternoon.* Her thoughts are constantly of self, while Juliet's thoughts are not of self.

Harry Morgan is another who concerns himself with a just punishment. He thinks, "So, Mr. Beelips, what the hell did he expect? That comes from playing at being tough. that comes from being too smart too often, Mr. Beelips." [40] He got what was coming to him, according to Harry. With this knowledge Harry still pursues the path of destruction, carrying the revolutionist robbers to Cuba. His moral code begins to restore itself as he views the needless killing of his friend Albert. He feels good kicking the machine gun over the side, but it is too late. Ignoring God's plan, he has taken his life within his own hands. He is going to make up for the loss he suffered when Mr. Johnson ran out on him. He kills a man, contemplates killing his rummy friend, and ends up fighting a useless battle against the revolutionists. His final affirmation, as quoted previously, is that "A man has no chance alone."

This could be interpreted to mean that a man has no chance without the help of fellow man or it could mean, more specifically, without the help of God. Man has paid for his sin. In *Green Hills of Africa*, Hemingway questions whether his own badly broken arm is his punishment for killing animals. Brett, in *The Sun Also Rises*, keeps repeating, "Don't we pay for the things we do, though?"[42] Here retributive justice is at its height. She can't bear to ruin another life, even though her life is past reclamation.[45] Santiago also realizes that he cannot go it alone. He needs the help of a fellow man and the guidance of God. The problem of sin and his lack of understanding of it keeps recurring to Santiago.[43]

Ernest Hemingway quotes F. Von Logau's remark on retribution in his small book *Three Short Stories and Ten Poems*, "The mills of God grind slowly, yet they grind exceedingly small." Harry Morgan, in "The Snows of Kilimanjaro," has a moment in which he sees the hideousness of Helen feeding upon everything that is dead in him, and he realizes that his misfortune might be his punishment for wasting his talent. Here again the woman is comparable to the hyena. He died spiritually when he relinquished his integrity for security.

Hemingway, the man, felt humility also. He enjoyed the humble, simple people and did not seek glory for glory's sake. Many accounts are told of his relation with the common people of Cuba and the lumbermen of Michigan. He always seemed to echo the cry, "I am not worthy, Lord." His own failure to understand his position is irony, and he used irony in some of his writing. His insight into it is humility. He regretted the shortness of time allotted to him to accomplish all God had intended for him, and he speaks of this in three of his major writings.[44] This horrible searching and yearning to

48

be all that God had intended made him, at times, an impossible man to live with. His four wives testify to this fact. He explains in *Across the River and Into the Trees* that Richard Cantwell loved too deeply and possibly demanded too much.

Hemingway's objectivity was a quality which stimulated his capacity for humility. No subject was too lowly for his attention; no person was too minor for his interest. Attempting to maintain complete objectivity, he was an advocate of simplicity. Hemingway believed, and his characters portrayed, the idea that a writer should be completely humble. He said, "Once you put a thing in letters, unless you do it on your knees, you kill it." [45] Hemingway did not pose as an authority or a judge. He said, "Let those who want to save the world if they can see it clear, do it." [46]

In a letter to Max Perkins, Hemingway said, "I am not a Catholic writer, nor a party writer, nor even an American writer, but just a writer meant to rise above injustice." [47] Hemingway claimed that a writer is forged in injustice and is made to suffer, as Dostoevsky for instance, suffered in Siberia. This adds emphasis to the previous discussion of the Hemingway characters crucified in the world.

Many incidents in Hemingway's life bear out his conviction of the need for humility. When he won the Nobel Prize for Literature in 1954, for instance, he told the first reporters who interviewed him that there was another writer more worthy than he, and this writer was Carl Sandburg. [48] Leicester Hemingway records that Ernest gave the medal and the money to the Shrine of the Virgin de Cobra in eastern Cuba, maintaining that "Nobody really had anything until it was given away." [49]

Milt Machlin refutes this in his book, *The Private Hell of Ernest Hemingway,* saying that he sent the money to his son John. Hemingway, in his life and writing, echoes the observation of Walter Chalmers Smith:

> And all through life I see a cross
> Where sons of God yield up their breath;

49

There is no gain except in loss;
There is no life except by death
There is no vision, but by faith.[50]

His dependence on those he loved is revealed in a telephone conversation with Carl Sandburg. He then said, "I am lonely. Miss Mary is on a train from New York to Minneapolis for a visit with her mother. I'm sort of helpless without her." Even Max Eastman, who often did not agree with Hemingway, notes his humility in Hemingway's comment, "I'm scared to death," and says, "Hemingway won my affection in his attempt to conquer this fear." [51] Another point Hemingway made was, "No writer can ever write anything truly great when he feels superior to the people he is writing about, no matter how much compassion he has." [52]

Of all the critics who testify to Hemingway's humility, Joseph Conrad, John Peale Bishop and Alfred Kazin have made three of the most significant statements on this point. Joseph Conrad records this statement of Hemingway, "We used to say the first lesson that an author has to learn is that of humility: to write as humbly as possible." [53] Hemingway was humble toward his craft and demanded discipline and work, necessary ingredients in making a humble writer. John Peale Bishop said, "Toward his craft, Hemingway was humble and had moreover the most complete literary integrity it has ever been my lot to encounter." [54] Kazin noted that Hemingway railed at Sherwood Anderson for his lack of humility and emphasized Hemingway's remark that only those who see so much more deeply than most men can feel will be successful writers. Man must be helpless. A complete surrender is necessary in his aimless perpetual reaching. Kazin concludes that if Hemingway had not sought so much he could not have been humiliated so deeply.[555]

Hemingway felt that belief should not be made too complex. With a "winner-take-nothing" attitude, the Hemingway characters approach God as helpless children, uttering childish beliefs and remembering childish prayers. One remembers the

Bible passage: "Except ye be converted, and become as little children, ye shall not enter the kingdom of heaven." [56] And yet, a simple faith is extremely difficult. Richard Cantwell states, "I might run for a Christian in the end." In other words, he didn't know if he were good enough for the position or if his preparation of suffering would be considered adequate. "For inasmuch as Christ suffered for us in the flesh, he must likewise suffer." [57]

Wrestling within the framework of liberal Protestantism, participating in World War I and returning to face the hedonistic life of the 1920's, Hemingway through stark realism attempted to formulate a moral code to replace the idealistic morality of his boyhood. If there is a wrong, right it; if there is disease, cure it; if there is suffering, endure it; if there is death, meet it courageously. The act of meeting each challenge makes man more than an animal, if somewhat less than a god: and Hemingway accepted this challenge.

CHAPTER III

HEMINGWAY'S CATHOLIC TRADITION

Hemingway's religious thought gravitated from the pole of belief in a Protestant tradition toward the pole of disbelief, skepticism and disillusionment, and then, in 1928, toward the pole of belief in Roman Catholicism. Ernest's conversion to Catholicism came as a result of his second marriage, to Pauline Pfeiffer, a Roman Catholic.[1]

Ernest Hemingway expressed many Catholic beliefs in connection with his father's suicide in that fateful year of 1928. Two of his notable Catholic tendencies were his belief in the Mass and purgatory. Marcelline Sanford speaks of Ernest's acceptance of the Mass, saying, "He told us he had had a Mass said for Daddy, and he led us in the Lord's Prayer before the services." [2] Leicester Hemingway expresses Ernest's belief in purgatory by quoting what Ernest said in an aside at the funeral, "If you will really pray as hard as you can you'll help get his soul out of purgatory. There are plenty of heathens around here who should be ashamed of themselves. They think it's all over and what they don't seem to be able to understand is that things go right on from here." [3]

It is important to note that a belief in purgatory offers hope for suicides. The Catholic belief also would support the possibility of mental derangement, to alleviate the mortal sin. Yet the attempt to justify his father's action haunted Hemingway throughout his entire life, for he believed that a Christian must pay for all his sins.

Hemingway's concern about the morality of suicide grew from this point on. In *For Whom the Bell Tolls,* Robert Jordan recalls an earlier suicide as he contemplates an attempt, concluding that Grandfather would not have been pleased with such a lack of courage. The old man, in "A Clean, Well-Lighted Place", has attempted suicide a week before and now sits searching for the light in a meaningless world. In the short story "Fathers and Sons," Nick believes that the life his father lived helped to set the trap for suicide. The thinking of these characters parallels the thinking of Hemingway, the man. Suicide, to Hemingway, was a cowardly hyenic death. In *Death in the Afternoon,* Hemingway states that he considers suicide banal and says that a bullfighter is cheating when he looks for death.

After his father's death, Hemingway sought a divorce from his second wife, Pauline, who was granted custody of their two sons. Infatuated by the vivacious, talented Martha Gellhorn, Hemingway proposed marriage, and the two were married by a justice of the peace in Cheyenne, Wyoming. The short story "Wine from Wyoming" was possibly inspired at this time. Affirmation that he remained a Catholic is found in this story:

> "It's not good to change one's religion."
> "I stay a Catholic." [4]

The Church, not recognizing the divorce, placed a penalty of excommunication on Hemingway. Excommunication is a denial of privilege concerning the Mass, but it does not cut the member off from the Church. Despite the penalty, a member is still bound to his obligations to the Church as a Catholic. Therefore, Hemingway remained an excommunicant of the Roman Catholic church. Leicester Hemingway claims that Ernest wanted a clean break with Pauline and with the Catholic church,[5] and that he had requested the address of an uncle, William E. Miller, who had written many hymns in the Episcopalian hymnal. Whether Hemingway wrote to him for advice or not is not recorded. Ernest succeeded in having Martha Gellhorn divorce him in 1945, but his break with the Catholic church is not mentioned. Hemingway remained attached to the Catholic church through the years after his fourth marriage to Mary Walsh and continued a Catholic until his death on July 2, 1961.

His own experience running parallel to his father's, Ernest Hemingway, who had diabetes in addition to various other illnesses, began to suffer from deep depression, which, medical authorities agree, is typical of a diabetic. Hemingway died, as did his father, of a gunshot wound, and was buried in the Ketchum village cemetery located beneath the Sawtooth Mountain he loved. Father Waldmann, officiating at the funeral, read the first chapter of Ecclesiastes, at the request of Hemingway's wife, and concluded, "Beneath it [the earth] rests the body of a Basque shepherd." Because of Hemingway's excommunicated state, he was denied the privilege of the complete funeral Mass.

The question of why Ernest Hemingway deserted American Protestantism to embrace Roman Catholicism has interested critics for a long time. Catholicism may have attracted Hemingway because it was a broad, ancient tradition which seemed to be more refreshing than its anemic offshoot: idealistic American Protestantism. Catholicism offered Hemingway an opportunity to explore the very root of Christianity.

Hemingway was also attracted to Catholicism because of its practical and realistic approach. Too many American Protestants had retreated to an "ivory-tower" type of religion. Others had complacently placed their hope in another life, regarding this life as a vale of tears in which happiness could not be expected, because they were all guilty. Detaching themselves from the earthly world, Protestant ministers placed erring man so far below them that they lost contact with the human element in their faith. Hemingway was repulsed by this lack of humility. The Protestant ministers were no longer a ministry which helped lift the common man but one which judged him unjustly. On the other hand, the priests met erring man on his level, divested of a "holy" or "fatal" view. They accepted God's creation, man and the universe, as good and, with this positive approach, ministered to man's needs through boundless love. Hemingway deserted Protestantism because it

54

seemed to him to be a religion founded on fear, while Catholicism was founded on love.

A tremendous amount of religious unrest accompanied the 1930's, and thus Hemingway's action also could be said to be typical of the times. "On the eve of the thirties," Kazin writes, "writers were turning to new faiths." [6] T. S. Eliot, a writer whose religious poetry influenced Hemingway, had embraced Anglo-Catholicism. Eliot's joining the Catholic tradition was an act of profound humility that grew out of the momentous experience of the charities of life.[7] Mr. Pritchett has called T. S. Eliot a Puritan, a cosmopolite searching after the older European culture: the older, richer tradition. Eliot knew the unbridged gulf between the Church and the world, and he said, "Christianity will continue to modify itself into something that can be believed in." In spite of their belief in the broad, Catholic tradition and its more practical approach to life, Hemingway and Eliot would have had to recognize that liberal Protestantism remained the only religion capable of arriving at the great solutions of ethics and religion. Catholic dogma and priest-interpreted scriptures would continue to thwart their progress. Protestantism restricted the physical being but encouraged the mental being through its use of the "Open Bible."

The discipline and ritual of the Catholic faith likewise appealed to Hemingway's deeply rooted puritanical sense of order and control. Throughout history, religious rites have been recognized as capable of disciplining the mind. From the pagan incantations to Christian liturgy, people have felt the need for disciplined repetitive actions. Altar preparation became honored as a purging, cleansing and disciplining force, making man capable of communicating with a Supreme Being. Possibly it was because of an ancient, crying need in the soul of man that Hemingway was attracted to the Mass, which represented the tradition of form and discipline that Protestant churches had modified or, in some cases, abolished. Ernest Hemingway felt the need for an empathic response to life and the religious situation.

55

In his writing Hemingway explored the power of rituals. Nick Adams, in "The Big Two-Hearted River," relives the Creation as part of his ritual of growing up. Philip Young feels that the story is an incantation of evil, but the predominance of "good" throughout the ritualistic preparation of a youth in the wilderness seems to be Nick's preparation for the lessons of God.

Great concern with order, tradition and hierarchy were in part a result of Hemingway's direct and constant perception of disorder or unknowable order. His inner violence was connected with a formidable assertion of order. Nick Adams is similar to Isaac Compson in William Faulkner's novel *The Bear*. Both are involved in the rites of puberty. From the ritualistic youth in the wilderness, in "The Big Two-Hearted River," to ritualistic bullfighters, in *Death in the Afternoon,* to ritualistic drinkers, in *For Whom the Bell Tolls,* to ritualistic lovers, in *Across the River and Into the Trees,* Hemingway expresses concern over the value of discipline.

Depicting a completely Catholic atmosphere, Hemingway's stories of France, Italy and Spain are dominated by Catholic references. The only book written in the pre-Catholic tradition is *in our time*. Catholic symbolism permeates his writing largely because of the setting. Catholic medals, priests, festivals of the Church, the young boy Paco who dies before performing an act of contrition, the young girl who cannot marry because of an act of the Church and the prayers of the Mass are all incorporated in his themes.

Hemingway's treatment of the Catholic church is one of respect. In *A Farewell to Arms,* Lt. Henry does not bait the priest but admires him because he has the true faith, which is not a "dirty joke." Mr. Frazer respects the nun, in "The Gambler, the Nun, and the Radio," because she has God. Richard Cantwell respects the people of Torcello, who built a church to worship their God. Hemingway respects the truth, and he respects these people because their sincerity comes nearest the truth. Significantly, this same respect is not shown in the Protestant references in his earlier stories.

56

In the light of these persistent impulses towards Catholicism, Hemingway's conversion becomes clearer. The ethics of Catholicism included elements of human nature which were omitted in Hemingway's American environment. His American background withheld from him freedom of thought, knowledge and spiritual values necessary for his central purpose. The hope he found lacking in the fatalistic attitude of Protestantism of the 1920's was inherent in Catholicism. Christianity, Hemingway thought, should be a religion of joy, not one of puritanical gloom. Early twentieth-century Protestants seemed to forget that they were creatures immersed in a good creation. The struggle Hemingway experienced was in overcoming the fatalistic doom, the hell and damnation of a Jonathan Edwards.

Hemingway's rebellion against American Protestantism resulted from his conception of the Protestant church in America as a false pietism, a combination of legalism and religious sentimentality which was lacking in many particulars, namely, a positive interpretation of bodily life and the life of the sexes, and a regard for God-given intelligence. He found the Protestant church obscurantist and narrow ("God Rest Ye, Merry Gentlemen," "Mr. and Mrs. Eliot"), and pictured it as living in naive and hooded ignorance of the tide of social forces. He and many others unjustly considered the Protestant church groups, as Matthew Arnold would have called them, Philistines. The efforts of the churches on behalf of the workers, for instance, in the steel strike of 1922, were ignored. This rebellion was motivated by ethical protest, not a desire for license.

One of Hemingway's major themes, which evolved out of his conversion, was that of remorse and humiliation. This did not lead to censure in Hemingway's writing, for to censure others is to dissociate ourselves from them and relieve ourselves of responsibility. Hemingway stressed man's responsibility and expanded this theme in the novels *For Whom the Bell Tolls, The Old Man and the Sea* and *To Have and Have Not.* The change one witnesses in his writing, beginning with his short-story collection *in our time* and the novels *A Farewell to Arms* and *The Sun Also Rises,* and culminating in *For Whom the Bell Tolls, The Old Man and the Sea* and *To Have and Have Not,* is significant to his conversion. Hemingway's inherent hope is coupled with his realization of man's responsibility to man. To Hemingway, it mattered a great deal how man lived his life here on earth. In *Green Hills of Africa,* he says you are responsible for every damned thing you do. This idea of good works is strictly a Catholic view, which contrasts with Calvinistic predestination, and a portion of this belief found expression in the simple statement, "God helps those who help themselves."

Man could approach the final step with the courage and honor characteristic of a noble death, or he could approach the final step with the "messiness" characteristic of an ignoble death. The Catholic church holds that the purpose of life is death, and that the aim of a good man on earth is to save his soul in the next world. The ultimate truth of Ecclesiastes is, "The day of death is better than the day of birth." Following the further reasoning that birth is receiving and death is giving, Hemingway's acceptance of death as a gift is understandable. Wisdom is defined basically as the comprehension of death, and "no young man believes he shall ever die." Contrary to this immature belief, man will die, and he is a responsible agent who must accept that responsibility. Hemingway supported this belief in his writing. He firmly believed that one had to lose his soul to gain it, give away the gift to have it and all his later writing rings with the acceptance of responsibility for his life and the lives of others.

The priest, in *A Farewell to Arms,* verifies a similar belief, explaining, "When you love you wish to do things for. You wish to sacrifice for, you wish to serve." Hemingway characters—like Robert Jordan, testifying that no man is an island; Santiago, testifying that no man can kill his brother and live on the sea; Harry Morgan, testifying that no man has a chance alone; and Philip Rawlings, testifying to comradeship—magnify this belief.

58

Hemingway's negative view of life in *in our time, A Farewell to Arms* and *The Sun Also Rises* presented evil at its apex. This is not a fatalistic view of human life, founded on the belief that the inherent evil in man renders life meaningless, but rather negativism softened by the hope discussed previously. Negation in the form of pessimism or bitterness, which some critics see in *in our time, A Farewell to Arms* and *The Sun Also Rises,* is far from fulfilling the conditions of religious insight. The irony of *in our time* is modified if one reads the Collect for Peace directly following the quotation "Give us peace in our time, O Lord," for it states:

> O God, from whom all holy desires, all good counsels, and all just works do proceed; Give unto thy servants that peace which the world cannot give; that our hearts may be set to obey thy commandments, and also that by them, we being defended from the fear of our enemies, may pass our time in rest and quietness; through the merits of Jesus Christ, Our Saviour. Amen.[8]

Thus, it is obvious that Hemingway was aware that there is no peace on earth.

In most of his writing Hemingway is not negative but hopeful, as is exemplified, in the short story "Indian Camp," by the sun that rises as the father and son row home from the tragedy of birth and death, and by the abiding qualities of the earth. Hemingway's extreme love of life led him to believe that God's initial intent was that creation be good. The Protestant code of morality, which evolved from a predominantly negative view, was an impossible code to follow, while the Catholic code, which evolved from a positive view, was more applicable to a practical life.

Surpassing all the stated reasons for Hemingway's conversion to Catholicism was his marriage to a Roman Catholic. Mixed marriages were frowned upon by the Church, and the only way to appease the churchmen's anger was for a Protestant to become a Catholic. Despite his conversion, Hemingway remained a freethinker in regard to religion in this new Catholic tradition, as well as in the Protestant tradition. He was not bound by the belief of the Church, but accepted those views which were compatible with his thinking and rejected others. His character, Richard Cantwell, for instance, accepts the love of the girl, Renata, who cannot marry him because of the tenets of the Catholic church. Cantwell obviously did not accept the Church's position on divorce, nor did Hemingway. Cantwell often ponders the Catholic religion, revealing a belief in mortal and venial sin.

Hemingway's freethinking views are reflected in the speed with which he recognized corruption in the Catholic church of Spain during the Spanish Civil War (1936-39). In 1931 the republican reforms in the Spanish Government included a separation of Church and state. According to the new constitution, "The Spanish state had no official religion." [9] Yet the peasant classes of Spain had been oppressed by slavery, due to the ancient tradition of Church dominance. The populace was downtrodden, while the monasteries enjoyed extreme wealth. The revolt often resulted in the burning of churches and convents, and these acts of violence were often interpreted as a persecution of Christianity.

This, however, is far too simple a view of the Spanish Civil War, just as the view of fascism versus communism fails, under analysis, as an explanation. The Nationalists represented the monarchists, large landowners and the Roman Catholic church. The Loyalists represented the laboring classes, who feared a return of slavery, and included many true Catholics who wished to restore true faith in the churches. Communism and fascism remained the radical minority in these groups. Hemingway sided with the Loyalists to the end, but was not one of the minority groups. It is incorrect to assume that because Hemingway was against fascism, he was for communism.

In his narration for the film "The Spanish Earth," Hemingway speaks of the superior military force of the Franco army as "mechanized doom." [10] The Loyalists surpassed the Nationalists in numbers but lacked the assistance which had been afforded to the opposition. The moral problem was always how much you were holding the people back by a just and necessary prudence. Hemingway concluded that death was still badly organized in war. Its "messiness" made it immoral by his code.

Hemingway's wife, Pauline, did not agree with his position on the Spanish Civil War [11] but remained loyal to the edict of Pope Pius XI, who condemned the legislation separating Church and State. Anselmo, in *For Whom the Bell Tolls,* refers to the State church as dead, and Jordan calls him a true Christian. Hemingway's Protestant tradition is firmly in the foreground in this decision. His Protestant and democratic belief supported the separation of Church and State. Hemingway's liberal religious view is best expressed in his comment, "I am not a Catholic writer." [12] He wrote the truth as he saw it not as it was interpreted for him.

Hemingway's ideal was "grace under pressure." All his stories are about the difficult acceptance of what the self sees to be the true nature of experience and about the achievement of grace, under pressure of that reality, if you are lucky enough to support some passion. Mizener concludes, "No wonder Hemingway for a long time tried to think of himself as a Catholic." [13] It would not do to force a conclusion, but one could say that Hemingway accepted much of the Catholic tradition, as well as much of the Protestant tradition, leaving unheralded his disbelief.

CHAPTER IV

HEMINGWAY'S GENERAL RELIGIOUS VIEW: CHRISTIAN VIRTUES AND CHRISTIAN SYMBOLS

Hemingway was always reticent in talking about sensitive beliefs, which he felt were destroyed or cheapened by this action. Jake's statement to Brett is a good clue to Hemingway's reticence on this subject of spiritual states. Brett explains that her experience in relation to Romero, the Spanish bullfighter, is a spiritual one. Jake tries to shut her up and says, "You'll lose it if you talk about it." States of the spirit are fragile and tenuous, and the less said about them the better, lest they be cheapened and lost. Man is given to spiritual vanity-words. Religious experiences always left Hemingway feeling awkward and embarrassed.

Ernest Hemingway's writing is, like all American literature, rich in Biblical imagery. His very style, admittedly, is patterned after the repetitious simplicity of the Old Testament. It is not mere coincidence that Hemingway's character in *in our time* is named Nick Adams, which suggests "old Nick" and "Adam", or good and evil. His story is the story of the fall of man, the battle of good against evil. He presents an attitude balanced between the positive and the negative. Everything that God created is good. The abuse of creation is evil.

The first book of Genesis catalogues Creation and after each day concludes with, "And God saw everything that He made, and behold, it was good." A parallel exists between this first book of the Bible and the story of Nick Adams' preparation of his place in the wilderness.[1] Throughout the entire account, Nick is reliving Creation. He uses the word "good" repeatedly until he gets to the "good place."

As Nick walked, he noticed that "underfoot the ground was good walking." [2] As Nick lay down, "the earth felt good against his back." [3] In preparing his bed, "his hands felt good from the sweet fern." [4] Finally, "now things were done, it was a good place to camp. He was there in the good place." [5] This reference to the "good" of Creation continues throughout the story, and its recurrence is far too frequent to be coincidental.

All of Hemingway's writing gives similar proof of his belief that Creation is essentially good. The basic hope that is present in most of his writing is derived from this concept. Significantly, *in our time* ends with the hope present in "The Big Two-Hearted River." Despite the predominant evil in *The Sun Also Rises,* the reminder is that "the earth abideth forever." [6]

Hemingway's belief in truth and light is another proof of the positive value, hope eternal. Hemingway writes about death and violence, but underneath it all is a recurrence of "light" symbols. In "A Very Short Story," the name of the girl is Luz (light), and she comforts Nick during a time of fear and loss. Praying in a Duoma, a Catholic cathedral, he has "light" near to him, and yet he must go on searching. She cannot be his. Nick is always happy in the "light", as illustrated in the dazzling whiteness of "Cross-Country Snows." In "Now I Lay Me", Nick needs a "light" to reassure him that his soul will not leave his body.

The mountain-home image, Carlos Baker suggests, represents man, God and home in "A Clean Well-Lighted Place." [7] "The Snows of Kilimanjaro" is the best example of this belief. The light-and-home symbol is the snow-capped mountain: Masai, Ngaji, Ngai, the House of God. Carlos Baker suggests that Hemingway was using Psalm 121, namely, "I will lift up mine eyes to the hills," as a basis for this work. R. O. Stephens, in his article "Hemingway's Riddle of Kilimanjaro," relates the search of the frozen leopard for light and home. [8] No one could explain what it was doing at that altitude (Hemingway's reference for this incident was the book entitled *Across East African Glaciers,* by a German geographer, Hans Meyer.).

Use of religious names, such as Swahili (mountain spirit

of Ngara), Kilimanjaro (male spirit inhabiting the mountain), Kibo (bright western peak) and Mawenzi (dark eastern peak), add other rich symbols. Harry Morgan dreams that he reaches the snow-white top of the mountain. It is an attempt by man to transcend his animal nature and reach a spiritual plane of existence. The brown of the mountains, in *A Farewell to Arms,* stands as a reminder of a foreboding gloom which is the result of retributive justice. This is one of the few Hemingway novels which does not end on a note of hope eternal.

In *Death In the Afternoon* the *toreros* receiving top billing fight during the day and the second rate *toreros* fight during the night. In "A Clean Well-Lighted Place," an old man is comforted by the light. The old waiter, attempting to pray with the light off, finds that the words mean nothing without the "light." With the light back on, the waiter says, "The light is very bright and pleasant but the bar is unpolished." [9] The symbol is complete: the light, bright and high, represents home; and the bar, spotted and low, represents evil on earth. The "Light of the World" shows the man going in a different direction from the whores, which illustrates an individual choice of God and home.

The dominance of the Gospel of St. John can be felt throughout this persistent use of light symbols. "The life was the light of men . . . the light shineth in the darkness . . . sent to bear witness of the light . . ." etc. God is light and truth, and truth is knowledge. In "The Gambler, the Nun, and the Radio," or as it was originally called, "Give Me a Prescription, Doctor," everything, including religion as known on earth, is considered the opium of the people, the only exceptions are revolution and knowledge, and knowledge is God.

Thus it can be seen that Hemingway makes much use of the day-and-night, light-and-dark symbolism. In *Death in the Afternoon,* the *top rated toreros* fight during the day and the second-raters at night. Philip Rawlings, who promised to marry Dorothy one night, says in the morning, "Never believe what I say at night. I lie like hell at night." Religion also is a night-thought to Robert Jordan. The conclusion suggests that light is goodness and darkness is evil. Light and darkness can also be paralleled with birth and death. Birth, coming from the dark into the light, is a sort of death, for as soon as we are born we begin to die; and death, going from the light to the dark, is a sort of birth into eternal life.

Allusions to Our Lord run through *Across the River and Into the Trees,* "Today is Friday," *The Old Man and the Sea,* "God Rest Ye, Merry Gentlemen" and the little story first published in *The Double Dealer,* "Divine Experience." *The Old Man and the Sea,* abounding in religious symbolism, is built on Christian virtues. The obvious symbolism requires no explanation. Santiago is a fisherman teaching the young boy the humility necessary for a good life. During his trials with the fish, his hands pain him terribly and his back is lashed by the line. He hooks the fish at noon, and at noon of the third day he kills it. As the second and third sharks attack, the Old Man utters "Ayee." Hemingway comments that "There is no translation for this word and perhaps it is just such a noise as a man might make voluntarily feeling the nail go through his hand into the wood." [10] The Old Man shoulders his mast and goes upward from the sea, being forced to rest seven times. When he reaches his cottage he lies on his bed "with his arms out straight and the palms of his hands up."

The Christian symbolism shifts from man to fish, and the confusion is consistent with the Hemingway philosophy of sacrificer and sacrificed and with formal Christianity as well. Furthermore, the phenomenon closely parallels the Roman Catholic sacrifice of the Mass, where a fusion of the priest-man with Christ takes place at the moment of transubstantiation.

Even the numerology used includes key numbers from the Old and New Testaments: three, seven and forty. Santiago had fished for forty-four famine days and forty more with the boy. The trial with the fish lasted three days. The fish was landed on the seventh attempt; seven sharks were killed; the Old Man rested seven times, while Christ rested three. Through these references one realizes that Hemingway is consciously aware of God and a crucified Christ.

Hemingway possessed many Christian virtues. Throughout his life and in his writing, the Hemingway image is one of compassion for his fellow man. From the separate peace of Nick and Lt. Henry to Philip Rawlings, Robert Jordan's "no man is an island," Santiago's "no man is ever alone on the sea" and Harry Morgan's "no man has a chance alone," one senses a deepened awareness of the relation of an individual to God and his fellow man. The English restraint of *in our times,* which leaves one repeating, "I guess it was a bit of a war," makes one scream with compassion, the intended response. Robert Jordan draws parallels between the Spanish Civil War and the American Civil War, illustrating man's inhumanity to man. One is made to feel compassion for whores, soldiers, drunkards, bullfighters and priests in this gigantic "Human Comedy."

Hemingway is remembered as a gentle, honest bear of a man.[11] The haunting refrain of "Onward, Christian Soldiers" is heard in his 1922 cable from Adrianople: "In a never-ending staggering march the Christian population of Eastern Thrace is jamming the roads towards Macedonia." Hemingway's concern for humanity is illustrated by his willful participation in many wars. As a volunteer in the Italian Army during World War I, he risked his life at the front and witnessed much pain and suffering. The Turkish-Greco campaign inspired his reports of the dead in harbors and of pack animals with their legs broken, left to drown. The retreat from Caporetto, in *A Farewell to Arms,* is illustrative of another example of inhumanity.

Hemingway's short story, "A Natural History of the Dead," reveals with bitter irony that part of the picture which a naturalist like Mungo Park forgot. What beauty could be seen in Nature when it included the bloated bodies of the dead? As a war correspondent in World War II, Hemingway managed to be on the first boat crossing to Normandy on D-Day.[12] His compassion is further born out by beliefs such as the one in "A Dangerous Summer," when he had quit praying for himself during the Spanish Civil War and only prayed for others. After the terrible things he had seen happen to other people, he felt that it was egotistical to pray for himself.[13]

In *For Whom the Bell Tolls,* the inhumanity of the Spanish Civil War is stressed by the union of the two opposing forces in prayer. It is in death, in the act of truth, where these parallels are best seen. Joaquin switches his thoughts from the Communist, La Passionaria, to Mary, as he approaches death. Later, when Lieutenant Berrendo begins to pray for his dead friend Julian, he prays "Hail, Holy Queen," [14] and Anselmo, praying for the partisans who had killed Julian and were in turn destroyed by Berrendo likewise turns to the Virgin,[15] concluding with the closing words of the "Salve Regina," the opening words of which had been uttered by Lieutenant Berrendo. Two men, each from opposing forces, pray one prayer from beginning to end.

Colonel Richard Cantwell, in *Across the River and Into the Trees,* teaches the youthful Renata that "dying is an egotistical ugly process." One becomes concerned with self, which diminishes the stature of a noble man. Cantwell claims Renata is too young to know such compassion. The old Colonel's bitterness has resulted from having to kill when he didn't hate. Killing was particularly repulsive to him, because, as he said, "Nobody ever killed them in Mass as we killed Krauts before they discovered Einheit." [16] Colonel Cantwell quotes Rommel as saying, "I love my enemies sometimes more than my friends, love with swollen hands and all my heart." [17] Hemingway's vision expands to include compassion for cripples. Cantwell loves Arnaldo, who has a glass eye; Renata loves Cantwell's crippled hand, because it is symbolic of his suffering in the world.

Hemingway's honesty is one of his most admirable virtues. Whatever his associates thought of him personally, whatever they though of him critically, agreeing or disagreeing with each other, they all are in agreement on the integrity of Ernest Hemingway. He lived honestly and wrote honestly. His writing lives as a testament to his truth and simplicity.

In a statement about writing, Hemingway claimed that a

writer needed the honesty and probity of a priest.[18] This was Hemingway's major criticism of Tolstoy's writing, for he said that the thought in Tolstoy's *War and Peace* was ponderous, Messianic thinking which was no better than that of an evangelical professor of history; and, therefore, he began to mistrust his own thinking.

His characters testify to this same love of truth. Renata, in *Across the River and Into the Trees,* claims that each new day was a disillusion, and Colonel Cantwell hastens to correct her, saying that each new day was a wonderful illusion that must be stripped of its falseness. In *For Whom the Bell Tolls,* Jordan speaks of his father as a religious and sincere man. He is embarrassed by the damp, religious sound of prayer, and he says, "Sincerity left one feeling awkward." [19]

Hemingway ridicules the honesty of the Neo-Thomists in his ironical "Neo-Thomist Poem." [20] He twists the psalm to read, "The Lord is my shepherd, I shall not want him for long." Much of his ironical writing presented the idea that things may not be what they seem through a double-exposure kind of scene, as in *in our time.* Hemingway would say, as his character Richard Cantwell says, "Liars lie best in a little smoke or when the sun has set. The hard light demands the truth."

Hemingway's absolute refusal to accept injustice proclaims his partial acceptance of the virtue of justice. Justice is a vague, nebulous term and can mean many things.[21] Hemingway questioned the varied meanings of the term and at times seemed to question whether God *was* just. Such questioning must culminate in a spiritual position. If Hemingway believed, as the rebels do, that God is murderous, he could not see any justice. If, on the other hand, he believed as a Christian that God is the ultimate ruling force in the universe, bringing good out of all the evil which He allows to afflict men, he could understand justice. Hemingway accepted the existence of injustice as did Camus, but maintained a hope that he would be able to see the justice of God, while Camus denied the existence of God. Hemingway explores this problem of justice in war, sports, hunting and writing. He concludes that writers are forged in injustice, a necessary evil.

Hemingway explores the virtue of patience through a consideration of man's ability to suffer and endure. Although he admires this virtue, it would be a fallacy to conclude that Hemingway was a patient man. He reacted too violently to too many situations to have earned credit for this virtue. Fortitude, on the other hand, is a virtue which Hemingway can honestly claim. He exhibited fortitude in all areas of his life: physical and mental. Hemingway believed that man must live his life in such a way that he exhibits honor and courage to his death. He must face each new challenge with firmness of mind in order to avoid a death without courage, which, according to Hemingway, is a "messy" death. Hemingway admired all who had lived and died courageously. He has written of the admirable courage of the bullfighters who daily faced death in the ring. Hemingway placed a high premium on self-control, conviction and personal courage.

The whole Hemingway man, legend and myth, is a man who grows through courage. "The Short, Happy Life . . ." is an example of man's search for courage. When Francis Macomber arrives at his goal and has sufficient courage to conquer the lion, he has become a complete man, master of his weakness. Hemingway has said that when man gains the necessary amount of courage, the world kills him. This story supports this conclusion. Macomber's wife, realizing that she can no longer dominate him, kills him. Although Hemingway recognized courage as a necessary ingredient of a noble life, he was not without fear. He devoted a lifetime to the study of its inception, growth and control. He felt, as Alexander Pope did, that it would be better to die than to live in fear. Proof of this is found in *Death in the Afternoon,* when Hemingway says that it would have been better had Gitanilla died, while he was still in control of himself and still had courage, rather than being forced to endure the progressive horror of physical and spiritual humiliation.

Besides courage, Hemingway stresses temperance, by exploring the results of intemperance: Intemperance, in *The Sun Also Rises,* led to unspeakable misery; in *Death in the Afternoon,* intemperance in sexual relations led to disease; [22] and fornication, in *Across the River and into the Trees,* led to hell. [23] In "The Snows of Kilmanjaro" intemperance destroyed Harry Morgan's talent (laziness, sloth, snobbery, pride, prejudice, by hook or by crook). Carlos Baker states that Hemingway's central theme in "The Snows of Kilimanjaro" is the same as that of Henry James in "The Lesson of the Master." In James' story, Henry St. George cautions, "Don't become in your old age what I have in mine . . . the depressing, deplorable illustration of the worshipper of false gods, idols of the market, money, luxury, every one which drives one the short and easy way." [24] Luxury ruined the people of wealth in Hemingway's Key West story *To Have and Have Not.* In a final note on intemperance, Hemingway says, "We destroy writers. They make money." [25]

The application of prudence throughout Hemingway's life made him very productive. His well-disciplined habits of writing perfected his skill. Throughout his writing, Hemingway shows that disciplined lives lead to happiness, and undisciplined lives lead to chaos and destruction. One of Hemingway's characters stated, in *Death in the Afternoon,* "If you disobeyed one of the rules, they killed you." The moral problem Hemingway discussed in his narrative "The Spanish Earth" was concerned with a just prudence. It is not enough to possess scientific "know-how" unless its discoveries are governed by a great moral "know-how."

In answer, then, to many critics who fail to understand Hemingway's religion, Carlos Baker says, "If Hemingway's work seems non-Christian despite the grave allusions to Our Lord, this is chiefly because he has refrained from taking doctrinaire sides in all his dramatizations of religious motifs. Consciousness of God is in his books, and *The Book of Common Prayer* was seldom out of his reach." [26] Hemingway's books are a living testament to a personal God he knew well.

If one chooses to criticize Hemingway for neglecting to affirm his faith, one must also recognize that he never denied his faith. It is true that Hemingway characters often claim nonadherence to religion, but at no time do they deny the existence of God.

CHAPTER V

HEMINGWAY, THE MAN, AND
HIS RELATION TO DEATH

Ernest Hemingway loved life, and in answer to critics who accused him of searching for death, he said, "Can you imagine that a man who sought death all his life, could not have found it before the age of fifty-four?" [1] It is one thing to be in the proximity of death and know what it is and another to seek it. His zest for life is the antithesis of the wish for death. Although life is a tragedy, Hemingway and his characters felt that it was worth living and fighting for. Jake Barnes spoke of getting his money's worth. Cantwell speaks of the luck he has had, which permitted him four chances.

Furthermore, it is not strange that Ernest Hemingway should be interested in exploring the mystery of death, in the shadow of the death of the Cross; but to say, as Professor Moloney did, that he described killing, death and suffering with a masochist's delight, is to force the meaning beyond intent. One need only remember that even though most churches preach the risen Christ, they dwell upon the passion of Our Lord and the crucifixion. Christ, in the words at the Last Supper, said to the disciples, "This do, as oft as ye think in remembrance of me." Protestants observe the passion of the Cross and the seven last words and permit the wearing of the crucifixion bier as a piece of jewelry. Catholics observe the fourteen stations of the Cross and enact the drama of Our Lord during this festival season. Therefore, although Hemingway explored death and was aware of the Christian preoccupation, he met life with a youthful, happy vigor, giving vent to his romantic nature, drawing great drafts of simplicity and beauty from the world.

Yet one cannot assume that his view of death was a Christian one, for he constantly challenges the paradox of the sacrificer and the sacrificed. Despite his writing about death, Hemingway never lost sight of the whole, or, as Richard Cantwell called it, "The Big Picture." [2] He wished to satisfy his curiosity, and his adventuresome spirit led him on his eternal search. His entire being was the embodiment of life: his clothing, his interest in the bull ring, the boxing ring and his actions in the hospital. His ready smile flashes in our memory.

Hemingway's living was symbolic of the times. The pace they drove was hard and fast. All his friends loved life, and all died before their time. Clark Gable, Gary Cooper, Humphrey Bogart, Tyrone Power and Errol Flynn are numbered among these close friends and played his heroes in his movies. Echoing through their lives is the saying, "Live while you live, and then die and be done with it," or, "Give a life this year and be quit the next."

Death remained as the supreme secret to Hemingway. [3] His character Richard Cantwell says, "The supreme secret is that love is love and fun is fun, but it is always so quiet when the goldfish die." In *Green Hills of Africa,* Hemingway says he always felt quiet when he saw an animal die. Hemingway continues to be thoughtful about death. Weiland Schmied was convinced that Hemingway did not seem to know death, although nothing interested him but death and its closeness. [4] In *Across the River and Into the Trees,* the old colonel carries death to a youth who derides him for his ideals. In *For Whom the Bell Tolls,* Pilar exemplifies the smell of death. But what death actually is, Hemingway does not know.

He explored God's plan for his life and searched beyond to glimpse a knowledge of death. Santiago's obsession is to catch the big fish. He believed that if one searched for truth one might get a glimpse of his eternal prize. Baker feels that the old fisherman tried to glimpse beyond. Santiago, carrying the mast crosslike up the hill, experiences the humility and love of Christ. The natural parable parallels the spiritual biography of "Samson Agonistes" and could be called "Santiago Agonistes." [5] Hemingway's theme concerns what is Christ-like in modern man. Somewhere between its parabolic and Christian meaning lies one important explanation of this book's power to move us.

Throughout life, Hemingway held that man was responsible for what happened to his life. God gave man a life, and what he did with his life was his concern. He could either use it wisely or abuse it. "Every damned thing you do is your fault." [6] Leo Gurko claims that Hemingway's characters, though often religious, have a religion that is peripheral, rather than central, to their lives. He explains that the fisherman relies on his own resources, not on God. After he succeeds he promises to say ten Our Father's and ten Hail Mary's and make a pilgrimage to the Virgen de Cobra. Gurko failed to read the informal prayers of Santiago throughout. These silent prayers of Santiago testify to a personal God, such as his utterance, "God let him jump". Santiago reaches a point where there is no time to pray, but he experiences the need of prayer, replying that he will talk to God later. Granted, Santiago is a strange mixture of religion and superstition (if you say a good thing it might not happen), but he is a typical representative of the Hemingway belief that religion is vain unless one is a doer, not a hearer. It would have been ridiculous to have Santiago, gripped by the tension of the situation, suddenly stop fishing and start praying. The simple proverb, "God helps those who help themselves," would explain Hemingway's theory of divine guidance. Practicality would not permit man to cease living and end life by praying.

Hemingway had a secret fear of the unknown "perils of the soul," which he felt could be alleviated through building an ecclesiastical wall between man and the unpredictable. As a young man, Nick felt his soul leave his body and was terrified. In an interview with Lillian Ross, Hemingway stated a Christian paradox, saying, "Only suckers worry about saving their souls. Who the hell should care about saving his soul when it's a man's duty to lose it intelligently, the way you would sell a position you were defending if you could not hold it as expensively as possible that was ever sold. It isn't hard to die." [7] Man must give his soul intelligently to God. Hemingway devoted much time trying to solve the dilemma which had arisen in his soul.

In his writing he gives evidence of struggling to find a belief in the hereafter or, as one might say, to add an eternal dimension to his life. He concludes that man's life does not end here on earth. Man proposes, God disposes; man aspires, God conspires. In *The Old Man and the Sea,* Santiago says that he cannot be defeated. Santiago survived defeat, spiritually and physically, in his three-day experience. Lt. Henry, in *A Farewell to Arms,* questions Greffi about his desire for life after death. Jesus, like some of Hemingway's characters, was destroyed by the sin of the world, but remained spiritually triumphant.

Hemingway's writing is of the perpetual "now," especially evidenced in *For Whom the Bell Tolls,* but one must not consider this neglect of future time as disbelief. Hemingway wrote only about the things of which he was certain. He suggests the existence of Hell, in *Across the River and Into the Trees,* when Colonel Cantwell tells Renata that he would be a guard at the gates of Hell. Cantwell adds, "To fornicate is forbidden and one can roast in Hell for it." The realization of Hell confirms the existence of Heaven. One cannot logically believe in Hell without believing in Heaven. Hemingway seems to believe, as was shown in his discussion with his brother, that "things go right on from here." His main problem is what goes on and if there is a hereafter; his doubt seems to be that he does not know if he will be accepted, the idea expressed in the political election, "I may run for Christian."

Because he is concerned about the hereafter, Hemingway recognizes the need of a Savior. Evidence of this concern is found in the quotation cited previously from *Across the River and Into the Trees,* "Speedy shrimp come to die for our benefit, O Christian shrimp, master of retreat, and did they not teach you about nets and that the lights are dangerous?" [8]

The question of the sacrifice and the sacrificer becomes

pertinent. This parallels the death of Christ, continuing with the thought of God's request. The Colonel buys six clams, which he cuts closer than necessary (taking all of his gift). He pays only a small pittance for them, but it is greater than the pittance received by those who caught them—(blood money received for selling Christ). The Jew, too, in "Today Is Friday," is interested only in the money received for the red wine (symbol of Christ's blood).

Hemingway uses literary references to make his reader aware of creation and death in his novel *Across the River and Into the Trees*. Colonel Cantwell questions creation through William Blake's poem "The Tiger": "What immortal hand or eye could frame thy fearful symmetry?" Cantwell says that the best way to die would be as in Whitman's poem "When Lilacs Last in the Dooryard Bloom'd," a tribute to a former commander in chief. Cantwell crosses over into the trees to rest awhile, as did a general before him, and a greater general, Christ, in Lanier's poem—"Into the woods my master went, clean, forspent, forspent." The closest Hemingway came to knowledge of death was that there were things for God to know and things for man to know, but if man went out too far, he was destroyed. The unrest of his soul found peace only in death.

Ernest Hemingway's faith was not a peace but a tragic hope, the essential ingredient in a Christian belief. There can be no faith without a struggle. His concern in life was not the summit but the fight for it, and the only battle worth winning was that against ignorance and fear. Although he felt his soul leave his body to commune with God, he could not conceive the vision of the hereafter. He maintained that there is no prize to be gained. The winner takes nothing, but gives a life of dedication and service to God. What God holds in store for us, after we have lived our life in such a manner as to satisfy God's intent, is the reward for the soul. Hemingway maintained, "You never have anything until you give it away." The soul cannot stay with the body, but is given to God through death.

Ernest Hemingway's writing will continue to endure because it is at once terrible and holy, a necessity of all primal fires, as John Ciardi said of Robert Frost.

As Morley Callaghan has said, "The older he got, the more often death kept hovering over his stories; he kept death in his work as a Medieval scholar might have kept a skull on his desk to remind him of his last end." [9]

CHAPTER VI

CONVERGING INFLUENCES

The complexity of Hemingway's religious and ethical position is reflected in the number of different movements with which critics have associated him. All are a part of the current of ideas which Hemingway's age inherited or are responses of his age to the world it inherited.

How man lives his life here on earth and how he meets death is one of Hemingway's main themes; but this man is not a Nietzschean superman or the superior being of Feuerbach's philosophy, as Professor Moloney suggests in his critical essay "The Missing Dimension." [1] Unlike the atheistic humanist, the Hemingway hero meets death with humility and courage, having achieved God's purpose here in life. Francis Macomber did not die before he had achieved this, nor did Robert Jordan. The Hemingway hero never denies the existence of God, while Nietzsche, defying the Christian belief that all virtue, all greatness of soul and all truths are gifts of grace, announced the death of God. This announcement became an agent in the quickening of the nihilistic forces which, in two World Wars, reduced the old liberal world to ruins.

Hemingway's story "A Clean Well-Lighted Place," when viewed objectively, represents this society of *nada*. An old man struggles to find meaning in the midst of a meaningless life. It must not be assumed that Hemingway accepts *nada* as a philosophy, but rather that he recognizes its force in the society of the day. The world inherited by the old man and the waiter is one of *nada*, and both of the characters react to it in different ways: The old man, failing in an attempted suicide, can find no answer, and is lost; likewise the waiter, a victim of the age

78

and philosophy, prays a bootless prayer and is equally lost. Light and "cleanness and order" are the only solution.

Hemingway intended the reader to feel the despair and nothingness of the age. A nihilistic society is usually found where men are filled with rapacity and sordidness. The result is demoralization through the garish seduction of materialism. Death is to be desired. Geismar, recognizing a death wish in Ecclesiastes, felt that this book paralleled the *nada* theory, namely: All is vain. Carried one step further, it can be concluded that the *nada* theory is dominant in *The Sun Also Rises*. This is true until the whole course of action changes with the inception of hope. Brett becomes capable of a moral act, and the earth abides forever. This hope and love of life, inherent in all Hemingway's writing, invalidates the charge that Hemingway was a nihilist who constantly wished for death.

Closely related to this hope is Hemingway's belief in immortality or a life in the hereafter. Professor Moloney stated that Hemingway's characters remained without faith in immortality, without mystery and without belief in salvation. This statement is contradicted by many Hemingway assertions, such as, "I liked bullfights because from watching them I got the feeling of life and death, mortality and immortality." [2] Nick speaks about his soul leaving his body, an immortal note. The belief of Santiago in the hereafter cannot be ignored. "But man is not made for defeat," Santiago said. "A man can be destroyed but not defeated. It is silly not to hope, he thought; Besides I believe it is a sin."

Continuing his concern about immortality in the autobiographical *Death in the Afternoon,* Hemingway speaks of the doctor keeping man alive, saying this man has an immortal soul and death would be the greatest gift one man could give another. In *Green Hills of Africa,* Hemingway reveals an irritation with the theatrical guide's comment, "It is finished." The novel ends on a note of watching and expectation. Hemingway questions why the grebes were not mentioned in the Bible story of Jesus walking on the Sea of Galilee. It is significant to remember that after the crucifixion, before Jesus ascended to the Father, He met with His disciples by the Sea of Galilee, telling them that He could not make them understand all, but with the coming of the Holy Spirit on Pentecost they would see more clearly. Hemingway's wife cannot seem to remember the face of a man with a beautiful soul, one visited by the Holy Spirit, and the final urgent command is, "You must."

Contrary to the second portion of the Moloney statement concerning lack of belief in salvation, Hemingway's writing provides evidence that he accepted the two premises upon which salvation is based: Christian concept of guilt, and strangeness of the mercy of God. Oppel, in his critical essay "Across the River," [3] also accused Hemingway of placing everything on being able to get along without a final significant principle to explain the metaphysical. But this is not the Richard Cantwell, who wonders whether he is worthy to run for "a Christian," or the Harry Morgan in *To Have and Have Not*, who realizes that man cannot take life into his own hands but is dependent upon a higher force aiding and helping him. Hemingway's nature admits a hope of salvation, for he refuses to accept the anti-Christian tenet of nihilism that man must refuse to struggle. If man is to remain a man he must meet every adversity. He must bring to life more than stoic endurance or the fatalistic attitude of the stoic. [4]

Hemingway refuses to accept the pessimistic attitude of the nihilist. He believes, optimistically, that there is a plan and that man alters the plan by his behavior. Accepting this view, Hemingway naturally rejected Dadaism—a movement closely associated with *nada*—which was popular during this period. He gives voice to his feeling through his character Harry Morgan, in "The Snows of Kilimanjaro," who speaks with contempt about the movement, saying, "And there in the café as he passed was that American poet with a pile of saucers in front of him and a stupid look on his potato face talking about the Dada movement with a Roumanian who said his name was Tristan Tzara who always wore a monocle and had a head." [5]

Dada rejected the entire world, but Hemingway's philosophy did not. Admittedly, Hemingway suffered from disillusionment after the war, but at no time did he completely reject society. To say, as Clifton Fadiman once did,[6] that Hemingway provided a violent romanticism for the lost souls, making lostness picturesque, is to misunderstand Hemingway's intent. The lost generation of the 1920's was the subject of Ernest Hemingway's novel *The Sun Also Rises,* but his lesson was not positive but negative. Hemingway is not disillusioned in *The Sun Also Rises,* but he writes of a disillusioned group. Yet, one finds great similarities between Hemingway and George Santayana's religion of disillusionment.

Santayana claims, with Hemingway's character Richard Cantwell, that all things are illusion. Nothing remains, absolutely nothing.[7] Man is confronted by a nothing that lives, and this is beautiful in its nothingness. The universe, apart from us, is chaos. Exercise of this power is the task appointed for us by the indomitable promptings of our own spirit, a task in which we need not labor without hope. We cannot change the world even if we boast of having made it; we must in any case learn to live with it. We must abandon our illusion to attain our ideals. Hemingway shows tendencies towards a similar belief. He too says. "Let those who want to save the world if they can, do it." Cantwell suggests that "Each day is an illusion to be stripped of its falseness."

Hemingway's view of life is the tragic nature of life; and because there is a certain amount of pessimism in his attitude, critics have associated him with the Naturalistic writers. Walter Fuller Taylor states that the writing of Hemingway is, on the whole, an expression of the Naturalistic view of man and the Naturalistic way of art—that, primarily, notwithstanding his late conversion to Catholicism and his occasional expression of some quasi-Christian attitudes.[8] Man's happiness, Hemingway assumes, habitually comes wholly from the expression and fulfillment of his natural self. Alfred Kazin's conclusion was that Hemingway's success could be attributed to a triumph in and of a narrow local and violent world and never superior to

81

it.[9] Carlos Baker referred to his Naturalism in his statement, "Here is nature and here is a man. Here also is something about the nature of manhood."[10]

But Naturalism places man too low on the creation scale. To speak of the Hemingway hero suggests that his action must be heroic and this conduct exalts man and does not fit the concept of Naturalism. Naturalism narrows man to an animal with no moral nature. But Hemingway is seriously concerned with sin and its effect on the moral nature of man, and there is no sin in Naturalism.

One must not lose sight of the fact that it is unwise to associate a writer too closely with his characters, and it is absolute folly to confuse the writer with these characters. Hemingway attempted to show characters who had lost the vision of the Almighty, but he did not intend to have them chronicle his faith to mankind. Many Hemingway characters claimed to have no religion, but one must not assume with finality that they did not believe. At no time in his writing do we read a complete denial of God. Robert Jordan believed in a union beyond life and, in his last moments, while contemplating suicide, decides to wait to die honorably. Love to him is immortal. He feels his soul slipping away. "He was completely integrated now and he took a long look at everything. Then he looked up at the sky. There were big white clouds in it. He touched the palm of his hand against the pine needles where he lay and he touched the bark of the pine trunk that lay behind."[11] Moments of indecision are not unnatural in times of extreme stress and suffering, and Hemingway accurately portrays this behavior. Besides claiming disbelief in the supernatural, Jordan questions, "Who am I talking to?" Christ also questioned during his passion, "Eloi Eloi, Sabachtani" (My God, My God, why hast Thou forsaken me?). Jordan's final prayer declares his belief, "Then let me last until they come." Hemingway's belief of a "right time to die" is completed in his character's prayer.

Hemingway further incorporates doubt of the supernatural in his stories, using Naturalistic ideas on several occasions.

In *A Farewell to Arms,* Lt. Henry watches the ants on a burning log. He contemplates playing the Messiah but throws water on them instead, which results in their death by steam. In "The Snows of Kilimanjaro," Helen is speaking in the supernatural realm when she questions, "Why did this have to happen to us?" Harry answers in pure Naturalism:

"I suppose what I did was to forget to put iodine on it when I scratched it. Then I didn't pay any attention to it because I never infect. Then later when it got bad, it was probably using the weak carbolic solution when the other antiseptics ran out that paralyzed the minute blood vessels and started the gangrene." He looked at her. "What else?"

Lt. Henry says:

"If people bring so much courage to this world the world has to kill them to break them—so of course it kills them. The world breaks everyone, and afterward many are strong at the broken places. But those who will not break are killed. The world kills the very good, gentle, and brave impartially. If you are none of these you can be sure it will kill you but there is no hurry."

In all these instances mentioned, the Hemingway characters are bitter. They are experiencing moments of skepticism, trying to reason logically what must remain as the strangeness of the mercy of God. They are fighting back against the inevitability of God's will. These moments are exemplary of the moments devoid of hope.

The most pure Naturalistic doctrine to be found in Hemingway is his attack on the anti-Naturalists in "The Natural History of the Dead." He replies cynically to Mungo Park's statement in which he questions, "Can the Being who planted, watered, and brought to perfection in this obscure part of the world, a thing which appears of so small importance, look with unconcern upon the situation and suffering of creatures formed after his own image? Surely not. Reflections like these would not allow me to despair. I started up and disregarding both hunger and fatigue travelled forward assured that relief was on hand and I was not disappointed." Hemingway refutes this statement by giving a realistic picture of the bloated bodies of the dead and men expiring in hideous ways—all from natural causes. Hemingway's argument is that one must be more realistic in determining the physical causes responsible for things in nature. He accuses Thoreau of inaccurate recording also, in *Green Hills of Africa*, saying that a Naturalist should have someone else record for him. Hemingway ridicules the sentimental idealism of the Naturalists just as he ridiculed the sentimental idealism of the Protestant church.

Despite Hemingway's obvious disdain for Transcendentalists like Thoreau (whom he cannot read) and Emerson, he is more closely tied to the beliefs of the Transcendentalists than to the beliefs of the Naturalists. Hemingway is unable to say with finality, as the American Naturalists do, that "Christianity is sham." [12] In spite of himself, Hemingway tends to agree with the romantics. Malcolm Cowley insists that Hemingway is only superficially a realist. His affinity to the Transcendentalists whom he often ridicules is far greater than previously supposed.

In *Green Hills of Africa*, Hemingway satirically states his admiration of the clean, dry minds of the Transcendentalists. But despite this satire, reference in nonsatirical instances to the "clean and dry" as a desired goal can be found in *A Farewell to Arms* and "A Clean Well-Lighted Place." The grandsire of Transcendentalism was the French Revolution; its mother, mystical philosophy; its father, the Puritan spirit. It was preserved from the morally unrestrained European romantic movement by its moral integrity.[13] Emerson and Hemingway shared similar beliefs in the midst of dissimilarity. Both being of Puritan background, they shared similar home atmospheres founded on hard work, discipline, self-sacrifice, independence, sincerity and realism. They admired similar virtues: self-reliance, directness and moral courage. Hemingway's basic moral code is directed by the same Protestant concept of conscience which Emerson upholds. Conscience is a divine, suprarational directive. Surrender to its impulses unites a person with God. This also is equivalent to the traditional concept of a mystical experience, an important ingredient in Transcendentalism.

Hemingway approaches such a belief in mysticism. A true mystic is one who believes in the possibility of union with God through spiritual meditation and submission. He believes that the ultimate truth may be grasped through spiritual intuition. In many stories Hemingway relates through his characters or his own experience the incident of the soul leaving the body and returning. His fear is the communing of that soul, and in these stories the act remains incomplete. In *Death in the Afternoon,* the doctor is operating on a man with an immortal soul. This belief in the immortality of the soul recognizes a communion with a Supreme Being.

The love affair between Robert Jordan and Maria approached mysticism also, as the world moved when the union was complete. A perfect union of love remains whole throughout eternity, and Robert Jordan assures Maria of their "oneness." The Spanish mystical tradition should not be ignored in its relation to Hemingway's belief. "She was La Gloria"; "I am no mystic but to deny it is as ignorant as denying that the earth revolves around the sun."

> For him it was a dark passage which led to nowhere, then to nowhere, then again to nowhere, once again to nowhere, always and forever to nowhere, heavy on the elbows in the earth to nowhere, dark, never any end to nowhere, hung on all time, always to unknowing nowhere, this time and again for always to nowhere now beyond all bearing up, up, up into nowhere, suddenly, scaldingly, holdingly, all nowhere, gone and time absolutely still and they were there, time having stopped and he felt the earth move out and away under them.[14]

The seventy hours of *For Whom the Bell Tolls* also has a mystical Biblical relation of three score and ten: living a full life in hours. Harry Morgan's feeling of soaring in a plane suggests a mystical ascension in "The Snows of Kilimanjaro."

85

This experience also is but a matter of hours. But Harry seems to be arriving at his goal after much striving. A timelessness seems to be associated with this mystical union. An entire lifetime passes in the space of hours. Complete communion is eternity.

The mysticism surrounding death concerned Hemingway also. He constantly searched for an understanding of an ecstatic moment in killing: a moment when man assumed the godlike attributes of giving death to free an immortal soul. Santiago's grave warning that it is not safe to discover the mysteries of God and the universe suggests that Hemingway realized that he should not violate the bounds of a God-dominated domain. Hemingway and Emerson recognized the correspondence between the human soul and all that exists in the world. Though the statement "God is in man and God is in nature" belongs to Emerson, it could belong to Hemingway. One of Hemingway's most consistent convictions was that, to the extent that man is in tune with nature, he fulfills the divine plan and his own proper destiny. He insists on the therapeutic value of nature, and his obsessive interests are those "natural" activities, namely, hunting and fishing.

Trying to cultivate the marginal life of the soul and recover himself in terms of the Catholic tradition, Hemingway found the mysticism surrounding the Catholic Mass appealing with its mystery of transubstantiation and the entry of the Holy Spirit. As the old Spanish tradition of mysticism could not be ignored by Jordan, the ancient Catholic tradition of mysticism likewise could not be ignored by Hemingway. Although Hemingway and Emerson rejected tradition, their "differentness" did not take on the characteristics of Thoreau. Hemingway concluded on several occasions that he was not able to read Thoreau. Hemingway, like the Transcendentalists, could not avoid the existence of the Creator in creation.

Because of his Transcendental attitude toward man and nature, many critics have mistaken him for a primitivist, a kind of Naturalist. Oscar Cargill claims that Hemingway was the first to make the public aware of primitivism.[15] Malcolm Cowley also attests that Hemingway is almost always described as a primitivist, finding a soul in every rock or tree. His preoccupation with ceremonies and rituals seems to be heralding from an ancient altar. Philip Young explores the heralding from an ancient altar in his discussion of "The Big Two-Hearted River." Zabel in *Literary Opinion of America,* has suggested similarities between Wordsworth and Hemingway on the grounds of romantic anti-intellectualism. But Hemingway was not a romantic Naturalist. He was more akin, as Malcolm Cowley suggests, to Poe, Hawthorne and Melville: haunted, nocturnal writers who dealt in images that were symbols of an inner world.

It is at this juncture that Hemingway and Emerson separate. Hemingway could not accept Emerson's belief that man was divine. He clung rather to the belief of man's close association with evil, as did the above writers, while Emerson clung to the belief of evil as man's sacred beneficent experience had by the laws of the universe. There is a temptation for many critics to associate Hemingway with a rankly negative school of existentialism, to class him among the philosophers of the absurd and nihilism.

The predominance of evil and suffering in Hemingway's themes has prompted this criticism. It is true that Hemingway recognizes evil and death, the first data of religion and morality, as a part of the abiding condition of man; but to say that he considers them to be the primary evidence of human existence, as the existentialist believes, is pressing the point. His arguments cannot be easily dismissed by a philosophy like existentialism. Christian faith is active in its cultivation of beauty and goodness, and sustained by the tragic hope in its acceptance of evil and death. Hemingway's belief is very like a tragic hope. For the Christians the ultimate character of the universe is good. For the existentialist, the ultimate character is evil and men are always uncertain. For Hemingway, the ultimate character of the universe is a balance between good and evil, and man is certain in his uncertainty. Existentialists, followers of the philosophy originated by Kierkegaard, feel

87

that man cannot know with any certainty what will become of him. No one can know his place or duty, but must take courage in hand and choose the best he can. He has no way of knowing if choice will bring salvation or damnation. The existentialist looks upon Sisyphus as the human exemplar, because of his disillusionment—hopeless and, therefore, still more courageous striving.

John Killinger, in *Hemingway and the Dead Gods,* explores the possible parallels between Hemingway and existentialism. He suggests that, for the existentialists, as for Hemingway's Nick Adams and Frederick Henry, the only peace in our time is the "separate peace," a nervous, tenuous half-peace which can be won only by the individual and must be won over and over again. The word "existentialism" is derived from the Latin, *ex stare* or *exsistere,* which means to "stand out." The basic attempt of all existentialism has been to establish the separate identity of the individual. Every man faces the choice of being a genuine individual or just a part of the crowd. He must make a choice to live comically, as the horse in *Death in the Afternoon,* or to live vitally, as the bull.

Through his existential choice, man takes on the godlike attribute of self-determination. The rapid advance of technological science, the devastation of two wars, the intellectual discrediting of traditional orthodox religion, all have spiritually and ethically marooned man. He must reconstruct a "separate peace."

As stated previously, in the review of Nietzscheanism and nihilism, nothingness is the convenient designation for the weirdness lying beyond the boundaries of existence and continually threatening to annihilate man. The Spanish word *nada* refers to this area of life once served by religion. The *nada* circle is present in the night fears of Jake Barnes and the "horrorous" of Philip Rawlings. The old patron and old waiter of "A Clean Well-Lighted Place" are united in nothingness.

Hemingway, according to Killinger, exalts the lone man. In Chapter VI of *in our time,* Nick is isolated. The superfluities of culture, race, tradition, even religion, all disappear in the face of one overpowering fact, the necessity to exist on an individual basis. Death and sin become synonymous. We never learn true worship until we learn to be alone before God.

Killinger considers *The Old Man and the Sea* as another separate peace. Santiago needs one catch in order for life to have meaning. On the contrary, Hemingway intended to point through Santiago that one cannot continue alone. He must depend on society and God for complete fulfillment. In his novel *Across the River and Into the Trees,* Colonel Cantwell, likewise, does not reject society, and fights all forms of bitterness. He is dying and must go alone, but his life lesson is given to Renata, and he feels that life has been good to him. He has been lucky. Carried one step further, absolute freedom is the freedom to kill and to take life, to assert oneself as an individual. But Hemingway was not a wanton murderer, but speaks of the art of killing. Santiago continually thinks of the sin involved in killing the fish.[16] The Hemingway man does not emerge timeless, godlike and free.

In "The Gambler, the Nun, and the Radio," according to Killinger, the opiates of the people are escape mechanisms. Granted that they are, but not for Mr. Frazer. Hemingway is again giving us his view of society. In *Green Hills of Africa,* Hemingway's individualism is seen in the statement, "It seemed too difficult sitting on a petrol case. People who lead complicated lives in religion, Rotary, etc., would sit that way." He prefers the ground. He continues his individuality in *Men Without Women,* saying that man is at his best without women. Despite these overt statements stressing individual choice, the Hemingway hero accepts his responsibility to society without the need of conformity. Hemingway personally participated in all wars and revolutions with a vitality which stands unequalled today. Exciting accounts of Hemingway on the beach of Normandy on D-Day are not the testimony of a man wishing to get out of things. *"In medias res,"* explains the man, Hemingway. If one were to pursue the reasoning of Killinger and a separate peace further, Hemingway would possibly be described as a conscientious objector, which is completely fallacious. He was surrounded by friends and enjoyed the activities of soldiers in the armed forces.

Nietzsche preached God dead when he found him so in the hearts and lives of contemporaries. Religion had become religiosity and the church a mere administrator of the sacraments. He descried as a holy lie that God who punishes, rewards in afterlife. Killinger confuses the disappearance of God and religion in his statement about *A Farewell to Arms*. In the book, Count Greffi asks, "Are you croyant?" and Lt. Henry answers, "Only at night." Count Greffi says, "Perhaps I have outlived my religious feeling." Lt. Henry says, "Mine comes only at night" [17] (when the mind is not clean and well ordered). It is not God who has disappeared here but religion.

John Killinger continues his defense, saying that war experience and death reduced Hemingway's morality from the complicated pharisaism of the 20th-century Church to the existentialism of Nietzschean ethics. War makes the urgency of the "now" responsible for the new views on morality in our time. Hawthorne is said to dramatize the human soul; Hemingway, on the other hand, relates the drama of its disappearance. War made traditional morality inacceptable. When God is overthrown and the world is without values, a rebel starts his own laws and moral code. God may have been overthrown for the world, but not for Hemingway, for in developing his code his Christian background is self-evident. Nicolai Hartman emphasizes in his famous work on ethics that anything which takes precedence over man in ethics, be it God himself, perverts it and makes it immoral. Man must rely on himself alone to maintain a sane median. To be moral is to discover fundamentally one's own being.

Hemingway comes closer to the description of a Christian existentialist who is constantly besieged by uncertainty, doubt and perpetual wrestling with the mystery of our final destiny. This new morality without eternity is probably closer to that of the Greek full life, in which one must live up to life and death. Hemingway supports the belief that all men are crucified by the world. Cantwell, Robert Jordan, Catherine and Santiago are such examples. There is no peace on earth. Man's continual striving is to form life out of a vast nothingness.

Killinger does include Hemingway's reversal of theme in the 1950's, but only to show the author's return. It is true that Hemingway rarely states views that are other-worldly, suggesting that he may not believe in eternity, but the very fact that he accepts the concept of the soul is sufficient to verify a belief in eternity. As a young boy, Nick feels his soul leave his body; the doctor, in *Death in the Afternoon,* operates on a man with an immortal soul; and finally, in "The Snows of Kilimanjaro," Harry says that "in some way he could work the fat off his soul the way a fighter went into the mountains to work and train in order to burn it out of his body." Even the Christian existentialists' view is far too narrow for the Hemingway belief.

Hemingway avoided overt Christian references because he feared the effect it might have on his writing: over-sentimentalized prose. The gospel authority would be glazed. W. H. Auden said, "Is there not something a little odd, to say the least, about making an admirable public object out of one's feelings of guilt and penitence before God?" [18] Then too, Hemingway's stories were extrovert in nature, with his interest centered on his fellow man. In "The Snows of Kilimanjaro," Helen says she wished he'd sometimes think of others; to which Harry Morgan answers, "That's been my trade" [19]—far from the solution of the "lone man."

CHAPTER VII

CONCLUSION

> It is the mark of a true novelist that
> in searching the meaning of his own
> unsought experience, he comes on the
> moral history of his time.
>
> John Peale Bishop [1]

Ernest Hemingway came, as all thinking men do, to the eternal question, "Why do I believe what I believe?" The things which he could solidly prove became the basis for his belief. The things he could not prove remained in that twilight area of question.

He had wrestled with the paradox inherent in Christian theology and understood it better than most men of his time. The basic anomaly in the relation of the Gospel to human culture is that it both condemns it and nourishes it. In the Scriptures and the early Church, a predominant negativism exists; and yet Jesus was able to recognize the beauty in natural objects as the beauty of "the lilies of the field." Paradox exists, for instance, in the saying of Jesus, "Do not swear at all, even by heaven, for it is the throne of God, or by earth, for it is his foot stool, or by Jerusalem, for it is the city of the great king." The letters of Paul present another paradox. A central Christian paradox is the apparent contradiction between the individual responsibility and divine sovereignty. "The greatest among you shall be your servant." "One must save life to lose it." Death of self is the beginning of selfhood.

There is an inherent danger in joining a writer with his

characters, and many Hemingway critics have fallen into this snare. When a thought becomes repetitious in a writer's work, however, it may be taken to represent an author's belief. Rising above his characters, and basic to his belief, Hemingway possesses an earthy Christian humility and sincerity. True to Augustinian tradition, the problem which really matters to Hemingway is the relation between the individual soul and its God. Abraham, Jacob and Moses become real to us because the problematic, bewildering aspects of life, as we know them, are present in their lives, too. Hemingway said, "I feared death until I realized that all men had experienced what I was experiencing."

One can derive from an author's writing his Christian understanding of man and the world. The Hemingway hero is an individual who is seriously concerned about the problem of good and evil, salvation and damnation. Having his traditional morality destroyed by war, the Hemingway hero is left to face a world without values, a world shrieking useless prayers to which the people do not listen. Hemingway's desire to find an honorable style of survival in a time of moral confusion indicates a certain strength of moral intent, a hope of preserving courage and dignity while experiencing a crack-up of values. He is a man in search of a moral style, as Romero, in *The Sun Also Rises,* holds the purity of his line through a maximum of exposure. Life consists in keeping an equilibrium with one's nerves and keeping a tight control over one's desires. He learns what he cannot have, as did Jake Barnes, who said, "I did not care what it was all about, all I wanted to do was live with it." [2] The human soul is stripped as it faces up to the ultimate challenge. The index to moral value becomes industry. Hemingway says, "Already, I am only happy when I'm working," which is repeated by Jake Barnes in *The Sun Also Rises.*

The main concern is life, here and now. It has been said that immortality as a spiritual concept devoted to life in the hereafter is not a real thing to Hemingway. "Only suckers worry about saving their soul. To save one's soul is less the problem than to lose it intelligently." [3] This should not be misinterpreted to mean that he does not recognize immortality, but rather that he recognizes and understands the Christian paradox. Jesus stated a similar paradox in the Gospel of St. Mark, 9:35: "For whosoever will save his life shall lose it; but whosoever shall lose his life for my sake and the Gospel's, the same shall save it." Hemingway saw this as a failing in others to "try to save their souls by what they write."

Bernard DeVoto argues that Hemingway does not treat the representative values of mankind. He says, "In short, the world most of us live in and the qualities by which we try to live are unrecognized in Mr. Hemingway's fiction, and he always attacked the life of the mind, the life of the spirit, and shared social experience of mankind." [4] On the contrary, Hemingway attacked merely what he found false in these lives. He was quick to give credit to honest endeavors and admired virtue when he found it.

Alfred Kazin's conclusion is that Hemingway's success is "A triumph in and of a narrow, local and violent world and never superior to it." [5] Carlos Baker, on the other hand, says, "Here is nature and here is man. Here is also something about the nature of mankind." [6]

Cleanth Brooks and Robert Penn Warren suggest, in "Discovery of Evil, an Analysis of 'The Killers,' " [7] that Psalm 121 could be taken as a motto for Hemingway's collected works (a belief they share with Carlos Baker):

> I will lift up mine eyes unto the hills,
> from whence cometh my help.
> My help cometh from the Lord
> Which made heaven and earth.
> He will not suffer thy foot to
> be moved; he that keepeth thee
> will not slumber.
> Behold, he that keepeth Israel
> shall neither slumber nor sleep.
> The Lord is my keeper; the

Lord is thy shade upon thy right hand.
The sun shall not smite thee
by day or the moon by night;
The Lord shall preserve thee
from all evil; he shall preserve thy soul.
The Lord shall preserve thy going out
and thy coming in from this time forth
And even forevermore.

D. S. Savage, in *A Withered Branch,* accuses Hemingway of seeing only the purposelessness of life and existence, and suggests that negation in the form of pessimism or bitterness is far from fulfilling the contention of religious insight. Aesthetic sensibility must be extended into spiritual perception, and spiritual perception must be extended into aesthetic sensibility and disciplined taste, before we are qualified to pass judgment upon decadence or diabolism or nihilism in art. To judge a work of art by artistic or religious standards, to judge a religion by religious or artistic standards, should come in the end to the same thing, though it is an end at which no individual can arrive.[8]

Hemingway, however, is hopeful even in his negative concept. He accepts responsibility in the face of evil. His characters do not measure up, as suggested, as creatures without religion, morality, politics or culture. Hemingway's search is a hopeful search for the plan of things. He does not present a picture of a man who has given up.

In an interview with George Plimpton, Hemingway said, "But you are more alone because that is how you must work and time to work is shorter all the time, and if you waste it you feel you have committed a sin for which there is no forgiveness."[9] In *Green Hills of Africa,* he is irritated by the words, "It is finished." He speaks of the short time remaining to achieve his purposes. Harry Morgan, in "The Snows of Kilimanjaro," is irritated with himself for squandering his talent. Time has run out for him. To Hemingway life has a definite plan and purpose, and it matters greatly what one does with his gift. Hemingway, it is true is no meliorist, and yet it is not just to say that he had the Spenglerian attitude that civilization is running down.

Man is capable of moments of illumination when the timeless touches, or intersects, the temporal. Experience is the preparation for the moment of intersection—to aid a person in his Christian faith and worship. Hemingway, like T. S. Eliot, felt that discipline, form and ceremony were necessary. The sacrament became an outward sign of an inward spiritual grace. The bartenders of Hemingway's stories become ministering priests at these rituals. "The Big Two-Hearted River" becomes more than the old romantic communing with nature. Nick undergoes purgation and preparation, which is followed by prayer, observance, discipline, thought and action.

Hemingway's entire religious experience was entered into in the spirit of criticism with moral overtones, which cannot be outraged without penalty. He maintained a passionate concern for justice, a sympathy for men, a sense of sin in a feeling of participation in a social wrong, and a belief in human values. This formed the warp and woof of his religious attitude to life. He was firmly grounded in the ultimate reality of God. He kept alive the earthy, humble note in literature and Christianity.

Walcutt, in his article in *Explicator No. 7*, sees the conflict in Harry's life as between a "fundamental moral idealism" and an "aimless materialism." [10] Physical infection, as a result of carelessness, is analogous to a spiritual infection from carelessness. The obvious parallel: Harry, working to remove the fat from his soul and working to conquer his infection, shows two imperfections which are to be the conditions of his death.

Hemingway's enlarged vision of good and evil is not cynicism but rather nearer to the classic attitude of Sophocles, to "see life steadily and see it whole." Man is not asked to retreat into some ivory tower for personal salvation. Hemingway seems to be certain of man's purpose in this world, but he seems to be in doubt about the other-worldly influences. It is this doubt which causes sleepless nights and statements con-

96

cerning nonbelief in the supernatural. What lies beyond in eternity cannot be proved but must be added as an eternal dimension to life. Socrates, likewise, did not have any certain knowledge of what would come after him.

Whether Hemingway accepted life beyond the grave or not remains a mystery, but it could be safely concluded that a belief in the supernatural—which Robert Jordan claimed you could not ignore, for it was as authentic as "La Gloria" or Johannes Sebastian Bach; Santiago could not do without; and Colonel Cantwell and Lt. Henry contemplated—remained as a tragic hope to Hemingway. The Hemingway here seems to say, "Help me endure, though I am not worthy, Lord." Hemingway testified to the existence of heaven when he said to Lillian Ross, "Italy was so damned wonderful it was sort of like having died and gone to heaven, a place you figured you'd never see." [11]

Hemingway, though true at times to both Protestantism and Catholicism, belongs not to one religion or one time but rather to a universal religion. This is stated by Colonel Cantwell, "The universal Chaplain of us all" must lead and guide man through this life in preparation for the next. Hemingway wrote of what he knew, not of what he anticipated. His novels dwelt on the persistent "now," leaving the future to the realm of questioning. His writing shows a discipline of intelligence and sensibility, being at both times both emotional and moral. Hemingway's writing is not a yearning for the past but the acceptance and development of a new pattern to be imposed. The pentecostal experience of love in *For Whom the Bell Tolls* is a surrender to a spiritual experience beyond us. It is the only alternative to consuming ourselves with sin and error. For a man convinced of the spiritual values, life is a coherent pattern where the ending has its due place; and because it is a part of a pattern itself, it leads into the beginning.

Anticipation of the hereafter is a pentecostal note in *Green Hills of Africa*. Watching by the Sea of Galilee, he remembers the miracle of Christ walking on the waters. His wife can't seem to remember the face of a man with a beautiful soul. One must remember and believe, lest Christ echo, "O thou of little faith, wherefore didst thou doubt?" Christ explained to the disciples that they would learn more from the coming of the Holy Spirit, for a man who possesses the Holy Spirit has a beautiful soul.

A cartoon in *The New Yorker* once showed a brawny muscle, knotted forearm and hairy hand clutching a rose. The caption read: "The Soul of Ernest Hemingway"—both beautiful and sensitive. Likewise, J. P.'s beautiful soul was not to be forgotten. There is a universality about Hemingway's religion as well as about his writing. His theme, like the theme of Dante, Milton and Bunyan, is one of Christian orthodoxy—man's trial in life treated in a nonorthodox manner. Hemingway, a creative soul confronting his times, develops this theme, striving to bring as much of our actual situation as possible into the light of expression and understanding.

Hemingway, in his own way, satisfied the necessary requirements of a dedicated Christian: a sense of awe in the majesty of God and a sense of his own unworthiness. His constant concern was to add an eternal dimension to his life.

NOTE

All references to the novels of Ernest Hemingway will be abbreviated in the footnotes in the following way after the first full citation:

Across the River and Into the Trees	ARIT
Death in the Afternoon	DA
A Farewell to Arms	FTA
For Whom the Bell Tolls	FWBT
Green Hills of Africa	GHA
in our time	iot
The Old Man and the Sea	OMS
The Sun Also Rises	SAR
To Have and Have Not	THHN

Notes to Chapter I

1. From *At the Hemingways'* by Marcelline Hemingway Sanford, copyright c 1961, 1962 by Marcelline Hemingway Sanford, reprinted with the permission of Atlantic-Little Brown and Company, Publishers.
2. *The Book of Common Prayer and Administration of the Sacraments and Other Rites and Ceremonies of the Church* (New York, 1945), p. 31.
3. Adelaide Edmonds Hemingway was a graduate of Wheaton College, a Congregationalist institution. She held a botany and astronomy major.
4. Ernest Hemingway, *in our time* (New York, 1958), p. 25.
5. *At the Hemingways'*, p. 102.
6. Ernest Hemingway, *A Farewell to Arms* (New York, 1952), p. 331.
7. Ernest Hemingway, *Across the River and Into the Trees* (New York, 1950), p. 193.

8. *At the Hemingways'*, p. 194.
9. It is interesting to note that Ernest Hemingway's son John was baptized as an Episcopalian. Recorded in Gertrude Stein's *Autobiography of Alice Toklas* (New York, 1933), she says, "Since all were of different faiths and none were practicing members of any church, it was decided to have John baptized Episcopalian (in England this is synonymous to the Anglican Church)."

Notes to Chapter II

1. Seymour Melman, *The Peace Race* (Ballantine, New York, 1961), p. 31. Reprinted by permission of Brandt and Brandt, New York.
2. Leicester Hemingway, *My Brother, Ernest Hemingway* (Cleveland, 1962), p. 72.
3. ARIT, p. 94.
4. Ernest Hemingway, *The Fifth Column and the First 49 Stories* (New York, 1938).
5. Ernest Hemingway, *Green Hills of Africa* (New York, 1953), p. 120.
6. Ernest Hemingway, *Death in the Afternoon* (New York, 1952), p. 223.
7. Milt Machlin, *The Private Hell of Ernest Hemingway* (New York, 1962), p. 185.
8. Ernest Hemingway, *The Old Man and the Sea* (New York, 1952), p. 116.
9. FTA, p. 191.
10. Delmore Schwartz, "Ernest Hemingway's Literary Situation," *Southern Review,* III (1938), pp. 772-776.
11. FWBT, p. 205.
12. St. Matthew 26:40.
13. Edmund Wilson, *The Shores of Light* (New York, 1952).
14. ARIT, p. 286.
15. FWBT, p. 198. Note also that Jake makes this same comment in *The Sun Also Rises* (New York, 1954), p. 31.
16. Ernest Hemingway, ed., *Men at War* (New York: Crown Publishers, 1942. Used by permission.) Introduction. Internal

quote taken from Shakespeare's "Henry IV."

17. *My Brother, Ernest Hemingway,* p. 103.
18. DA, p. 4.
19. Henri Peyre, "Camus, The Pagan." Yale French Studies, No. 25 (Camus Issue, Spring, 1960, pp. 20-25.) © 1960, Yale French studies.
20. *The Poems of Emily Dickinson,* Martha Dickson Blanche and Alfred Lute Hampson, ed. pp. 161-162. Boston: Little, Brown and Co., 1930.
21. Amos M. Wilder, *Theology and Modern Literature* (Cambridge, 1958). Due to circumstances beyond my control, I am unable to provide the page number of this quotation.
22. It was typical of the period for the young writers to flock to Europe and, particularly, Paris.
23. SAR, p. 43.
24. Alfred Kazin, *On Native Ground* (New York, 1942), p. 324. *Doctrine* (Baton Rouge, 1958).
25. DA, p. 59.
26. *Catholic Encyclopedia,* Vol. XIV, pp. 326-327.
27. Halford Luccock, *Contemporary American Literature and Religion* (Chicago, 1934), p. 274.
28. "The Land endureth forever."
29. GHA, p. 73.
30. Luccock, p. 274.
31. Quoted in Randall Stewart, *American Literature and Christian Doctrine,* p. 134. Baton Rouge: University of Louisiana Press, 1958.
32. Eugene Exman, "What is the Right Thing?" *Integrity and Compromises,* Institute for Religious Social Studies, Robert MacIver, ed. (1957), p. 112.
33. FWBT.
34. FTA, p. 259.
35. GHA, p. 95.
36. *House of Fiction,* Allen Tate, ed., (New York, 1950), pp. 421-423.
37. Robert Hart, "Hemingway on Writing," *College English,* XVIII, pp. 314-320.
38. Ernest Hemingway, "Now I Lay Me" *The Fifth Column,* p. 465.
39. Cf. p. 6, *supra.*

40. Ernest Hemingway, *To Have and Have Not* (New York, 1937), p. 161.
41. SAR, p. 26.
42. Cf. p. 24, *supra*.
43. Cf. p. 14, *supra*.
44. GHA; "Snows"; ARIT.
45. Pamplona Letter, *Transatlantic Review,* II, No. 3, as cited in Charles Simons, *Literary Views and Attitudes of Hemingway* (unpublished Ph.D. dissertation, University of Chicago).
46. DA, p. 279.
47. Personal letter, February 14, 1940, as cited in Simons, *Literary Views and Attitudes.*
48. Harry Golden, *Carl Sandburg* (Cleveland, 1961), p. 223.
49. *My Brother, Ernest Hemingway,* p. 249.
50. John Bartlett, *Familiar Quotations.*
51. Max Eastman, "Phoenix Nest," *Saturday Review,* March 24, 1962.
52. "Defense of Dirty Words," *Esquire,* September, 1934, p. 158.
53. Joseph Conrad, *A Personal Remembrance,* p. 207.
54. F. J. Hoffman, *The Little Magazine, A History and Bibliography* (Princeton, 1947).
55. Kazin, *On Native Ground.*
56. Matthew 18:3.
57. I Philippians 4:1.

Notes to Chapter III

1. Marcelline Hemingway Sanford reports this in her book, *At the Hemingways.* Leicester Hemingway in his book, *My Brother, Ernest Hemingway,* says, "Ernest, in a letter to his parents around 1925, casually mentions attending Mass." A statement in the *Autobiography of Alice B. Toklas* refutes this statement. Gertrude Stein speaks of Ernest's desire to have Miss Toklas and herself as godmothers of his son John. "Since they were all of different faiths and most not practicing, the baby was baptized Episcopalian."
2. *At the Hemingways',* p. 283.
3. *My Brother, Ernest Hemingway,* p. 99.

4. Ernest Hemingway, *Winner Take Nothing* (New York, 1933), p. 169.
5. *My Brother, Ernest Hemingway,* p. 200.
6. Kazin, *On Native Ground,* p. 239.
7. "Ash Wednesday" and "The Hollow Men," *Modern American Poetry,* ed. Untermeyer (1942), pp. 435-439.
8. *Book of Common Prayer,* p. 31.
9. E. A. Peers, *The Spanish Tragedy, 1930-1936* (New York, 1936).
10. Ernest Hemingway, *The Spanish Earth* (Cleveland, 1938).
11. Machlin, *The Private Hell of Ernest Hemingway,* p. 127.
12. Personal letter to Max Perkins, as recorded in Simons, *Literary Views and Attitudes.*
13. Mizener, *The Far Side of Paradise,* as cited in Simons, *Literary Views and Attitudes.* Morley Callaghan says that Hemingway felt good about being a Catholic. "He called himself a Catholic now because he recognized that he really had been Catholic for some time—by temperament . . . he was in fact intended to be a Mediterranean Catholic." *That Summer in Paris,* p. 95. New York: Coward-McCann Inc., copyright, 1963.

Notes to Chapter IV

1. "The Big Two-Hearted River," iot.
2. *Ibid.,* p. 182.
3. *Ibid.,* p. 183.
4. *Ibid.,* p. 185.
5. *Ibid.,* p. 186.
6. Cf. p. 67, *supra.*
7. Carlos Baker, *Hemingway, the Writer as Artist.* Princeton, N. J.: Princeton University Press, 1952.
8. R. O. Stephens, "Hemingway's Riddle of Kilimanjaro," *American Literature Quarterly,* Vol. 32 (March, 1960), pp. 84-87.
9. Hemingway, *Fifth Column* . . . , p. 477.
10. OMS, p. 118.
11. *Life,* July 14, 1961, p. 61.

12. "Hemingway's Longest Day," *True,* February, 1963.
13. *Life,* September 12, 1960, p. 78.
14. FWBT, p. 326.
15. *Ibid.,* p. 327.
16. ARIT, p. 230.
17. *Ibid.,* p. 286.
18. *Men at War,* Introduction.
19. *Ibid.,* p. 405.
20. *Collected Poems of Ernest Hemingway.* "The title 'Neo-Thomist Poem' refers to temporary embracing of church by literary gents."—E. H. The Thomist group founded by Etienne Gilson and Jacques Maritain applied the Thomist principle of the relation of grace and free will to modern economics, sociology and politics.
21. Camus has stated that man's justice is a vain thing. See *The Stranger.*
22. DA.
23. ARIT.
24. Carlos Baker, *op. cit.*
25. GHA, p. 23.
26. Baker, *op. cit.,* p. 259.

Notes to Chapter V

1. Ivan Kashkeen, "Alive in the Midst of Death," in Baker, *Hemingway and His Critics.*
2. ARIT.
3. Wieland Schmied, "Man Without a Twilight," *Der Vort.*
4. *Ibid.*
5. Carlos Baker, "The Marvel Who Must Die," *Saturday Review,* XXV, September 6, 1952.
6. GHA, p. 281.
7. Lillian Ross, *Portrait of Hemingway* (New York, 1961), p. 21.
8. ARIT, p. 193.
9. Morley Callaghan, *That Summer in Paris,* (p. 95) New York: Coward-McCann, Inc., 1963.

Notes to Chapter VI

1. Moloney, "The Missing Dimension," *O.M.S.,* pp. 103-105, 114-115.
2. DA, p. 18.
3. Oppel, "Across the River," in Baker, *Hemingway and His Critics.*
4. Carl Van Doren claims, in *The American Novel,* that Nick Adams followed a stoic code. D. S. Savage claims that the following passage from *A Farewell to Arms* is representative of fatalistic stoicism: "Often a man wishes to be alone and a girl wishes to be alone too and if they love each other they are jealous of that in each other, but I can truly say we never felt that."
5. Hemingway, "Snows of Kilimanjaro," p. 165.
6. Herbert Muller, *Modern Fiction: A Study of Values* (New York, 1937).
7. George Santayana, "Religion of Disillusionment," in *Interpretations of Poetry and Religion* (New York, 1957).
8. Walter Fuller Taylor, *The Story of American Letters* (Chicago, 1956).
9. Kazin, *On Native Ground,* p. 340.
10. Baker, *Hemingway, the Writer as Artist,* p. 298.
11. FWBT, p. 471.
12. Malcolm Cowley, "Nightmare and Ritual," in McCaffrey, *Hemingway, The Man and His Work* (Cleveland, 1950).
13. Yvor Winters, *In Defense of Reason* (Denver, 1943).
14. FWBT, p. 159.
15. Oscar Cargill, *Intellectual America: Ideas on the March* (New York), p. 777. 1941-
16. Cf. p. 14, *supra.*
17. FTA, p. 270.
18. W. H. Auden, *The Dyer's Hand* (New York, 1962), p. 458.
19. Hemingway, *The Fifth Column,* p. 151.

Notes to Chapter VII

1. "The Missing All," in McCaffery, *Ernest Hemingway, The Man and His Work,* p. 297.
2. Irving Howe, "In Search of Moral Style," *New Republic* (September 25, 1961), 145:21-3.
3. Lillian Ross, *A Portrait of Hemingway,* p. 36.

4. Bernard DeVoto, *Literary Fallacy* (Boston, 1944), p. 106.
5. *On Native Ground,* p. 340.
6. *Hemingway, The Writer as the Artist,* p. 298.
7. In Brooks and Warren, *Understanding Fiction* (New York, 1944), pp. 315-324.
8. T. S. Eliot, "In Hope of Straightening Things Out," in *Twentieth Century* (1962), p. 147.
9. In Baker, *Hemingway and His Critics.*
10. "Snows of Kilimanjaro."
11. Ross, *Portrait of Hemingway,* p. 21.

A SELECTED BIBLIOGRAPHY

Adams, J. Donald, "Ernest Hemingway," *English Journal,* College ed., 28:87-94 (February, 1934).

——————. *The Story of American Letters* (Chicago: Henry Regnery Co.) 1956.

Allen, Frederick Lewis, *The Big Change.* New York: Bantam Books, 1961.

Baker, Carlos, ed., *Hemingway and His Critics.* New York: Hill, Wang, 1961.

——————. *Hemingway, The Writer as Artist.* Princeton: Princeton University Press, 1952.

——————. "The Marvel Who Must Die," *Sat. Rev. Lit.* XXXV (September 6, 1952), p. 10.

——————. Personal letter to Mrs. Julanne Isabelle, December 4, 1962.

Backman, Melvin. "Hemingway, The Matador and Crucified," *Twentieth Century Views,* R. Weeks, ed. Englewood Cliffs, N. J.: Prentice-Hall, 1962.

Beach, Joseph Warren. *American Fiction, 1920-1940.* New York: Macmillan Co., 1941.

——————. *The Twentieth Century Novel.* New York: D. Appleton Century Co., 1932.

Beatty, Jerome, Jr. "Hemingway vs. *Esquire,*" *Sat. Rev. Lit.* XLI (August 23, 1958).

Beaver, Joseph. "Technique in Hemingway," *College English,* XIV (March, 1953), pp. 325-328.

Beebe, Maurice. "A Hemingway Check List," *Modern Fiction Studies,* February, 1955, pp. 30-31.

Bluefarb, Sam. "Sea, Mirror and Maker of Character," *English Journal,* XXLIII (December, 1959), pp. 501-510.

Bode, Carl, ed. *Great Experiment in American Literature.* Mizener, "The Two Hemingways," pp. 135-156; 1961.

Brée, Germaine, "Camus," *Twentieth Century Views.* Englewood Cliffs, N. J.: Prentice-Hall, 1961.

Brooks, Cleanth, and Warren, Robert Penn. *Understanding Fiction.* New York, 1944.

Brooks, Van Wyck. "Fashions in Defeatism," *Sat. Rev. Lit.* March 22, 1941.

Burgum, Ed. Berry. *The Novel and the World's Dilemma.* New York: Oxford U. Press, 1932.

Burhans, Clinton, Jr. "The Old Man and the Sea: a Tragic Vision of Man," *American Literature Quarterly,* 31 (1959-60).

Callaghan, Morley. *That Summer in Paris.* New York: Coward-McCann, 1963.

Cargill, Oscar. *Intellectual America: Ideas on the March.* (p. 777). New York: Macmillan, 1941.

Carpenter, Fred. "American Myth: Paradise to be Regained," *PMLA,* 1959.

Colburn, William E. "Confusion in a Clean, Well-Lighted Place," *College English,* XX (1958).

Colvert, James B. "Ernest Hemingway's Morality in Action," *American Lit.* XXVII (Nov. 1955), pp. 372-385.

Cotter, Janet. "The Old Man and the Sea: An Open Literary Experience," *English Journal,* LI (October, 1962).

Cousins, Norman. "For Whom the Bell Rings," *Sat. Rev. of Lit.* XLII (Aug. 22, 1959).

Cowley, Malcolm. *Exile's Return.* New York: Viking Press, 1961.

Daiches, David. "Ernest Hemingway," *College English,* II (May, 1941), pp. 725-736.

Dewing, Arthur. "The Mistake About Hemingway," *North Amer. Rev.,* CCXXXII (1931), pp. 364-371.

Dickinson, Emily. *The Poems of Emily Dickinson.* Martha Dickinson Bianchi and Alfred Leete Hampson. Boston: Little, Brown and Co., 1930.

Durkheim, Emile. *Suicide,* Spalding and Simpson, tr. Glencoe, Ill.: Free Press, 1958.

Eastman, Max. "Great and Small in Ernest Hemingway," *Sat. Rev.,* XLII, (April 4, 1959), pp. 13-15.

"Ecclesiastes," *King James Version of the Bible.*

Ehrenburg, Ilya. "Memoirs of Ilya Ehrenburg," *Soviet Review,* Oct. 1962.

—————. *People and Life, 1891-1921.*

Eliot, T. S. "Religion and Literature," *Literary Opinion of America,* ed. Zabel. New York: Harper Bros., 1937.

Evans, Oliver. "The Snows of Kilimanjaro," *PMLA,* 76 (1961).

"Existentialism," *Encyclopedia Britannica,* 1961, Vol. 8, 968A.

Farrell, James. *Literature and Morality.* New York: Vanguard Press Inc., 1945.

Fenton, Charles. *Apprenticeship of Ernest Hemingway.* New York: Viking Press, 1958.

Friedrick, Otto. "Ernest Hemingway: Joy through Strength," *American Scholar,* XXVI (Autumn 1957), pp. 470-518.

Geismar, Maxwell. *Writers in Crisis: The American Novel between Two Wars.* Boston, 1942, pp. 39-85.

Goddard, Harold Clarke. *Studies in New England Transcendentalism.* New York: Columbia Univ. Press, 1908, p. 217

Golden, Harry. *Carl Sandburg.* Cleveland: World Publishing Co., 1961.

Grebstein, Sheldon. "Controversy," *American Scholar,* 27 (Summer, 1958), pp. 229-31.

Gurko, Leo. "Achievement of Ernest Hemingway," *College English,* XIII, pp. 360-375 (1952-53).

Guttman, Allen. "Mechanized Doom: Ernest Hemingway and the Spanish Civil War," *Mass. Review,* Vol. I (1959-60), p. 541.

Hackett, Francis. "Hemingway: *A Farewell to Arms,*" *Sat. Rev. of Lit.,* XXXII (August 6, 1949), pp. 32-33.

Halliday, E. M. "Hemingway's Ambiguity, Symbolism, and Irony," *Amer. Lit.*, XXVIII (March, 1956), pp. 1-22.

Hanrahan, Gene, ed. *Hemingway: the Wild Years*. New York: Dell Publishing Co., 1962.

Hart, Robert. "Hemingway on Writing," *College English*, XVII, pp. 314-20. (March, 1957.)

Hartwick, Harry. *Foreground of American Fiction*. New York: American Book Co., 1934.

"Hemingway," *Life*, September 12, 1960; July 14, 1961.

Hemingway, Ernest. *Across the River and Into the Trees*. New York: Scribner's, 1950.

――――. "Dangerous Summer," *Life*, Sept. 5, 12, 19, 1960.

――――. *Death in the Afternoon*. New York: Scribner's, 1952.

――――. *A Farewell to Arms*. New York: Scribner's, 1948.

――――. *The Fifth Column and the First 49 Stories*. New York: Scribner's, 1938.

――――. *For Whom the Bell Tolls*. Scribner's, 1940.

――――. *Green Hills of Africa*. New York: Scribner's, 1953.

――――. *The Hemingway Reader,* Charles Poore, ed. New York: Scribner's, 1953.

――――. *in our time*. New York: Scribner's, 1958.

――――, ed. *Men at War*. New York: Crown Publishing Co., 1942.

――――. *Men Without Women*. New York: Scribner's, 1927.

――――. *The Old Man and the Sea*. New York: Scribner's, 1952.

――――. *The Spanish Earth*. Cleveland, Ohio: J. B. Savage Co., 1938.

――――. *The Sun Also Rises*. New York: Scribner's, 1954.

――――. *Ten Short Poems*. Paris: Contact Pub. Co., 1923.

――――. *To Have and Have Not*. New York: Scribner's, 1937.

――――. *Winner Take Nothing*. New York: Scribner's, 1933.

Hemingway, Leicester. *My Brother, Ernest Hemingway*. Cleveland, Ohio: World Publishing Co., 1962.

Hicks, Granville, "Hemingway," *Sat. Rev.* 44:15 (Jan. 14, 1961).

Hoffman, F. J. *Modern Novel in America, 1900-1950*. Chicago: Henry Regnery Co., 1952.

————, Allen, C., and Ulrich, C. *The Little Magazine, A History and Bibliography*. Princeton: Princeton Univ. Press, 1947.

Holman, Hugh. "Hemingway and Emerson," *Modern Fiction Studies*, III, pp. 12-16, 1956-57.

Howe, Irving. "In Search of a Moral Style," *The New Republic*, 145:21, S. 25, 1961.

"In Memoriam," *Sat. Rev. of Lit.*, July 29, 1961, complete.

Kazin, Alfred. *On Native Ground*. New York: Reynal and Hitchcock, 1942.

Kempton, Kenneth. *The Short Story*. Harvard Univ. Press, 1947.

Killinger, John. *Hemingway and the Dead Gods*. Univ. of Kentucky Press, 1960.

Knoll, Robert, ed. *McAlmon and the Lost Generation*. Univ. of Nebraska Press, 1962.

Levy, Alfred J. "Hemingway's *The Sun Also Rises*," *Explicator* XVII, Item 37, No. 5, Feb. 1959.

Light, James. "Religion of Death in Hemingway," *Modern Fiction Studies*, Vol. 7, pp. 169. (Summer, 1961.)

Lovett, Robert Morse. "Ernest Hemingway," *English Journal*, XXI (Oct. 1932).

Luccock, H. E. *Contemporary American Literature and Religion*. Chicago: Willett-Clark Co., 1934.

Lynn, Kenneth S. "Hemingway's Dangerous Summer," *Mass. Rev.* Vol. 2, 1960-61.

Machlin, Milt. *The Private Hell of Ernest Hemingway*. New York: Paperback Co., 1962.

Marcus, Fred H. "A Farewell to Arms, The Impact of Irony and the Irrational," *English Journal*, LI, Nov. 1962.

111

McCaffery, John, ed. *Ernest Hemingway, The Man and His Work*. Cleveland: World Pub. Co., 1950.

Melman, Seymour. *The Peace Race*. New York: Ballantine Books, 1961. (Brandt and Brandt, Agents.)

Millet, Fred. *Reading Fiction*. New York: Harper and Bros., 1950.

Milner-Gulland, Robin, and Levi, Peter, tr. *Yevtushenko, Selected Poems*. New York: E. P. Dutton and Co., 1962.

Moody, Campbell, "Nietzsche and the Academic Mind," *PMLA*, 1947, p. 1183.

Moynehan, William, "Martyrdom of Robert Jordan," *College English* 21,, p. 127. October, 1959.

Muller, Herbert. *Modern Fiction: A Study of Values*. New York: Funk and Wagnalls, 1937.

Nodel, Rabbi Julius. "Freedom's Holy Light," *Best Speeches of 1961*.

Orvis, Mary. *The Art of Writing Fiction*. Englewood Cliffs, New Jersey: Prentice-Hall, 1948.

Paul, Elliot. *The Life and Death of a Spanish Town*. New York: Modern Library, 1937.

Peers, E. A. *The Spanish Tragedy, 1930-1936*. New York: Oxford Press, 1936.

Prescott, Orville. *In My Opinion*. Bobbs, Merrill Co., 1942.

Redman, Ben Ray. "The Champ and His Critics," *Sat. Rev. of Lit.*, XXXIII (1938).

Ross, Lillian. *Portrait of Hemingway*. New York: Simon and Schuster, 1961.

"St. John," Gospel of. *Catholic Encyclopedia*, Vol. 16, 1951.

Sanderson, S. F. *Ernest Hemingway*. New York: Grove Press Inc., 1961.

Sanford, Marcelline Hemingway. *At the Hemingway's*. Atlantic-Little, Brown and Co., 1962.

Santayana, George. *Interpretations of Poetry and Religion*. New York: Harper and Bros., 1957.

Savage, D. S. *The Withered Branch, Six Studies in the Modern Novel*. New York: Pellegrini and Cudahy, 1948.

Schmied, Wieland. "Man Without a Twilight," *Wort In Der Zeit,* Heft 8, Aug. 1961, VII, Juhrgang.

Schwartz, Delmore. "Ernest Hemingway's Literary Situation," *Southern Review* III, 1938, pp. 772-776.

Shneidman, Edwin, ed. Norman Farberow, *Clues to Suicide.* New York: Blakiston Div., 1957.

Sickels, Eleanor M. "Farewell to Cynicism," *College English,* III, Oct. 1941.

Simons, Charles. "Literary Views and Attitudes of Hemingway," unpublished Ph.D. dissertation, University of Chicago.

Snell, George. *The Shapers of American Fiction.* New York: E. P. Dutton Co., 1947.

Snyder, Louis, ed. *Masterpieces of War Reporting.* New York: Julian Messner, Inc., 1962.

"Special Outdoor World of Hemingway," *Sports Afield,* Dec. 1962, p. 53.

Spock, "Morality Today," *Ladies Home Journal,* Dec. 1962.

Stein, Gertrude. *The Autobiography of Alice Toklas.* New York: Harcourt Brace, 1933.

Stephens, R. O. "Hemingway's Riddle of Kilimanjaro," *Amer. Lit.,* 28.

————. "Old Man and the Iceberg," *Modern Fiction Studies,* Vol. 7 (Winter), 1961-62.

Stewart, Randall. *American Literature and Christian Doctrine.* Baton Rouge: Louisiana State Univ., 1958.

Taylor, Walter Fuller. *The Story of American Letters.* Chicago: Henry Regnery Co., 1956.

"Unitarians," *Encyclopedia of Religion and Ethics,* ed. Hastings, Vol. 13. New York: 1927.

Van Doren, Carl. *The American Novel (1789-1939).* New York: Macmillan Co., 1940.

Warren, Robert Penn. "Introduction to *A Farewell to Arms.*" New York: Scribner's, 1929.

Weeks, Robert, ed. *Hemingway, Twentieth Century Views.* Englewood Cliffs, N. J.: Prentice-Hall, 1962.

Wilder, Amos M. *The Spiritual Aspects of the New Poetry.* New York: Harper and Bros., 1940.

──────. *Theology and Literature.* Cambridge: Harvard Univ. Press, 1958.

Wilson, Edmund. *The Shores of Light.* New York: Farrar, Straus, Young, Inc., 1952.

──────. *The Wound and the Bow.* Cambridge, Mass.: Riverside Press, 1941.

Winters, Yvor. *In Defense of Reason,* Univ. of Denver, 1943.

Yevtushenko, Yevgeny. *Yevtushenko: Selected Poems.* Robin Milner-Gulland and Peter Levi, translators. Harmondsworth, Middlesex, England: Penguin Books, Ltd., 1962. U. S. Agents: E. P. Dutton Co., New York.

Zabel, Morton Dauwen, ed. *Literary Opinion of America.* New York: Harper and Bros., 1937, rev. 1951.